A Sheltered Life

Heidi Myers
2360 Ethel St
Kelowna BC V1Y 8T3

A Sheltered Life

Take It to The Streets

Jeremy Reynalds

Copyright © 2013 Jeremy Reynalds.

All rights reserved. No part of this book may be used or reproduced by any means, graphic, electronic, or mechanical, including photocopying, recording, taping or by any information storage retrieval system without the written permission of the publisher except in the case of brief quotations embodied in critical articles and reviews.

WestBow Press books may be ordered through booksellers or by contacting:

WestBow Press
A Division of Thomas Nelson
1663 Liberty Drive
Bloomington, IN 47403
www.westbowpress.com
1-(866) 928-1240

Because of the dynamic nature of the Internet, any web addresses or links contained in this book may have changed since publication and may no longer be valid. The views expressed in this work are solely those of the author and do not necessarily reflect the views of the publisher, and the publisher hereby disclaims any responsibility for them.

Any people depicted in stock imagery provided by Thinkstock are models, and such images are being used for illustrative purposes only.
Certain stock imagery © Thinkstock.

Although based on actual people and events, the specifics of some of the events and locations depicted in this book and the names of the characters involved have been changed to protect their identity and save them from any embarrassment.

All scripture quotations, unless otherwise indicated, are taken from the Holy Bible, New International Version®, NIV®. Copyright ©1973, 1978, 1984, 2011 by Biblica, Inc.™ Used by permission of Zondervan. All rights reserved worldwide. www.zondervan.com The "NIV" and "New International Version" are trademarks registered in the United States Patent and Trademark Office by Biblica, Inc.™. All rights reserved.

Editorial assistance: Leonard G. Goss, GoodEditors.com

ISBN: 978-1-4497-9020-2 (sc)
ISBN: 978-1-4497-9021-9 (hc)
ISBN: 978-1-4497-9019-6 (e)

Library of Congress Control Number: 2013905852

Printed in the United States of America.

WestBow Press rev. date: 4/08/2013

Praise for Jeremy Reynolds' Previous Work

***10 Minutes* reviews**

I like the characters. It is good Christian storytelling that incorporates prophesy, faith, action, and principles. What more can you ask for in a book?

—Janet Denise Ganaway Kelly,
founder and CEO of Sanctuary of Hope

Jeremy Reynolds's first novel, *10 Minutes*, is a fast-paced thriller displaying how quickly one's life can change. This suspense-filled, page-turning adventure provides an intriguing look at broadcast journalism, both local and international. After finishing *10 Minutes*, you'll look at television news with a different perspective. Along with that, Jeremy weaves in some international terrorism, and betrayal of one's country and marriage vows—asking implicitly, "Where is faith when it matters?" Perhaps most importantly, Jeremy shows—in a way that will have you sitting on the edge of your seat—that in the span of a short amount of time, decisions we make can have long-reaching effects. I highly recommend this book.

—Dan Wooding, veteran journalist and
founder of ASSIST News Service

10 Minutes is about how the decisions we make in a split second can affect the rest of our lives and the lives of others. The story moves along smoothly detailing the life of news reporter Cameron. The story is interesting, compelling, and thought provoking. It's a story of redemption and makes you think of your own life and faith. I recommend the book as an enjoyable and thought-provoking read.

—Dawn Moreno, founder of Esoterica!

Homeless in the City II Reviews

Jeremy Reynalds is an iconoclast who has combined a genuine passion for the hungry, homeless, abused, and addicted with a creative ministry model in New Mexico. His books give a face to what is often a faceless problem in today's society. This chronicle of his conversion, calling, and creation of an important agency of service—plus his guidelines for setting up a gospel rescue mission—is a valuable read for all who want to follow his lead and demonstrate their commitment to Jesus Christ in a practical manner.

—John Ashmen, president of
Association of Gospel Rescue Missions

In this amazing story, author Jeremy Reynalds, who founded and runs New Mexico's largest emergency homeless shelter and was once homeless himself, shares how he rose from homelessness to the pinnacle of academia, earning a doctorate in intercultural education at Biola University in La Mirada, California. In addition, the book contains stories of the precious souls who have fallen on hard times (many of whom we pass by daily, often without a glance) and gotten back on their feet again with the help of the Lord at Joy Junction. Jeremy's story inspired and challenged me to pay more attention to the needy and oppressed among us. I pray that it will likewise encourage you.

—Dan Wooding, founder of
ASSIST MINISTRIES and ASSIST News Service

Homelessness in our country is a story about tragedy and hope. Dr. Reynalds weaves together this story beautifully. The power of his words, however, can be found in his compassionate acts.

—Joel John Roberts,
CEO of PATH Partners and publisher of inforumusa.org.

Reviews of other books

If anyone knows the ins and outs of homelessness and the solutions that will work, it is Jeremy Reynalds. I have grown to deeply respect his work and labor of love for the underprivileged and needy. I know this book will help keep a cause in the forefront of our national consciousness that needs our ongoing attention.

Once again, I applaud Jeremy's willingness to champion the rights of those who rarely have such an impassioned advocate.

—Mike Shreve, BTh, DD, director of Deeper Revelation Books, Triumphant Living Ministries, and Mike Shreve Ministries.

Jeremy Reynalds has a special combination of blunt realism and a relentless pursuit of sharing God's grace with those in need. I have no doubt that heaven is pleased by the work that Jeremy does, and this book is a reflection of his heart.

—Chip Lusko, pastor

This book will touch and impact your heart, changing your view of the homeless.

—Johnny Probst, chaplain and author of the Strangers and Pilgrims book series

We are so used to seeing the needy and homeless, that sometimes we don't "see" them. While their often pleading eyes beg for a touch, smile, a simple hello, or a cup of coffee, many times we just go on our own way. In this book, veteran homeless advocate, Dr. Jeremy Reynalds gives us a glimpse into their pain-racked world and reason why you need to respond with love to the many homeless people who live on the streets in your city. It is a book you won't put down.

—Dan Wooding, journalist and founder of ASSIST Ministries and ASSIST News Service

With the increasing need for charity for homeless people, Jeremy Reynalds and Joy Junction stand out as a leader and a protector of many. Jeremy writes about what we all fear could happen to anyone. He brings reality to the forefront in hopes to make changes for many.

—Larry Garrison, president of Silver Creek Entertainment

To say from the comfort of our own homes that the plight of the homeless is not our own negates the alarming fact that it *can* happen to anyone. Jeremy's story proves this to be true. And proves it can be overcome. We support Jeremy on his tremendous journey and support the work of his tireless organization, Joy Junction.

—Rabbi Jonathan Aaron and Michelle Azar Aaron, Temple Emmanuel Beverly Hills

Provocative and knowledgeable, Jeremy Reynalds speaks from years of experience in serving the homeless population in a practical, sensible, and compassionate manner. His yearning and passion leap from the pages, grip your heart, and motivate you to get in the game and join him in the immense battle that must be fought by all of us. This is a must-read for anyone with a heart of serving others. Open your mind and be challenged. Otherwise, stay on the sidelines and let life pass you by through your inaction!

—Jim Sandberg, Senior Pastor, Tabor Baptist Church, Muncie, Indiana

Acknowledgments

Since *The Sheltered Life* is the story of how the Lord worked in my life and how, in the midst of a very dark time, he personally reawakened his original calling in my life, it is dedicated to him. Without the Lord the ministry of Joy Junction would not have come into existence.

This book is also dedicated to the many homeless men, women, and families who have met their Lord and Savior Jesus Christ and experienced his compassion while staying with us.

Thank you to our staff who carry out the vision of Joy Junction on a daily basis.

My thanks also go to Dr. Bob Gassaway, formerly of the University of New Mexico, who has been a wonderful mentor and a good friend and gave me a lifelong appreciation of the importance of correct grammar.

Contents

Acknowledgments..ix
Homeless in America... 1
Faltering First Steps...17
The Promised Land... 28
When Vision Becomes Reality....................................49
The Homeless Speak.. 54
More Homeless Speak... 66
A Slice of Life at Joy Junction...................................103
God in the Details: Everyday Evidence around Joy Junction.......110
An Incredible Journey...116
Made Whole by Jesus..125
You'd Be Surprised Who Hates the Homeless....................139
Sunday Night on the Streets of Albuquerque....................142
A Day in the Life of Joy Junction's Kitchen Manager.............155
An Unscheduled and Extraordinary Day........................158
A Day in the Life of the Resident Services Manager at Joy Junction..161
The Lord's Land—and He Rocks It with a Gentle and Firm Hand...167
Too Few Evangelicals Practice the Compassion They Preach.......178
What's Ahead for Joy Junction?..................................181

Homeless in America

I was not on a mission for God. I was just a broke young Englishman stranded in the American Southwest. I had made it to the New Mexico–Texas border but ended up standing in the blazing sun for hours. Cars sped by, but none stopped. As the hours passed, I was getting more and more tired, so I left the highway and walked to a store. I wearily looked through a telephone directory and called the first church I could find. I then asked the man who answered the phone if he could help me find shelter. The man told me I was welcome to sleep on the church floor, but I would have to walk there—a distance of about five miles. Needless to say, walking that far on an unknown Texas highway was more than my body or spirit could endure. I thanked him and dejectedly hung up.

Walking back, I saw a restaurant that was about to close for the night. It didn't matter, because I had no money for food. I saw that behind the restaurant there was a storage shed filled with odds and ends, and I looked for something to sleep on. The only thing that looked suitable was a piece of fiberglass, and that was my bed for the night.

I woke up early the next day and headed down the highway again. Soon, a trucker stopped and gave me a ride to Phoenix. By this time, I was starving. Without me asking, the kind trucker shared his sandwiches with me.

Looking back all these years later, I see the Lord's hand in my life. Back then I was just another homeless person on the road, but today I am founder and CEO of Joy Junction, New Mexico's largest emergency homeless shelter. The transformation came through God's grace in my life.

Growing Up in England

My heart pounded as I lay in bed and listened to the muffled, angry voices coming from the living room. My mother and father were arguing again. About what, I did not know. I just knew they were fighting, something they did almost every night. I was eleven, and I hated listening to my parents' fights. I knew my mother was unhappy living with my wheelchair-bound father, diagnosed several years earlier with multiple sclerosis. On a number of occasions, she acidly told me that if my dad had not been sick, she would have left him. At other times Mom informed me I should be grateful she stuck around to take care of my older brother and me. Lots of parents would not have done that, she said. My mother only married my father because he told her he would apply for a commissioned officer's position in Britain's Royal Air Force. He failed to do so, and now, because of his disability, there was no chance of that. She felt cheated and angry.

As sharp tones filtered through the muffled voices, I focused on the one bright spot on the horizon: I would be leaving for boarding school in a few weeks. Initially, I looked forward to this as an escape, but later it became my own private hell.

At boarding school in Bournemouth, only about an hour's bus ride from my home on England's south coast, I was the routine victim of schoolboy pranks, such as having my bed short-sheeted. Days were filled with dread, as I worried about being laughed at for my stammering when asked to give an impromptu answer. If that wasn't enough, there was also the necessity of faking a sickness to escape the perils of hockey games, rugby football, cricket, or cross-country running—all nightmares for my unathletic body and so much fun for others to laugh at. I didn't seem to fit in anywhere, so I retreated into a world of books, where no one demanded anything from me. This traumatic time was perhaps the beginning of my shutting down emotionally. The pain of being continually taunted by a multitude of pampered and merciless British kids was too much for me to bear.

Ironically, my escape on many weekends was to go back to the home from which I had tried to escape. Perhaps I concluded that the tension at home was somewhat bearable compared to the abject misery I endured at school.

Admittedly, there were a few fun times at school. One early morning, all the kids in my dorm awoke at about two o'clock, buzzing with excitement. The chapel was on fire. Since a destroyed chapel meant no church services in the morning and maybe for a long time, the kids were elated. These chapel services were extremely boring for me—just something else in my life to be endured rather than enjoyed. The fire and the circumstances surrounding it were the talk of the campus, and did we love what we found out! The word was that the school chaplain had gone for an evening of entertainment in a nearby town. Returning to school (where he lived) in the early hours of the morning, he found the chapel on fire. This hip spiritual adviser had not gone to town dressed in robe and cassock, however. He dressed in full sixties regalia, including a Beatles-style wig and high-heeled boots. Naturally, we all thought this was hilarious. No one talked about anything else for days.

I scarcely remember anything about most of my classes and my teachers. There was one very memorable class I attended, however, even though I hated it. It was math class, and my teacher, a born-again Christian, is someone I have never forgotten. The last few math lessons of each semester were different. For a treat at the end of each term, this teacher asked if we would like him to read to us. Naturally we agreed, even though we thought his choice of books could have been improved (but then, anything beat math!). His readings of choice were evangelical Christian books, usually dramatic life stories about a hero of the Christian faith who had done exciting things for the Lord. While I did not at that time know the author of the Good Book, the stories were very gripping and easily held my attention.

I took it on myself to argue with this teacher about whether Christianity was relevant to culture. I was then a vegetarian, and I had read books showing that Jesus didn't eat meat, either. I used those books as weapons to argue with him, and I twisted Scripture in any way I could to persuade him. Instead of falling for my arguments, this godly man responded that the important thing was not what Jesus ate but what he had done for me on the cross. I responded by letting my long-suffering instructor know that Christianity was a crutch for old women and the intellectually feeble. How difficult it must have been for this man to deal with my obstinacy! Still, those powerful, end-of-term stories remained with me, as did my memories of this faithful, patient teacher.

I wanted to study sociology, a subject not offered at my boarding school, so I finished the last couple of years of my education living at home again. I still did not fit in. I attended a different school, with different people, but I encountered the same misery. I was desperately lonely and felt like an outsider again. I threw myself into my studies, and soon I adopted all the latest sociological buzzwords and phrases into my vocabulary. One such phrase was Karl Marx's well-known saying, "Religion is the opiate of the people."

I remember scoffing at various religious posters I saw plastered around town. I proudly declared, "I am not a Christian. I am an agnostic. You can't tell if there is a God." My mother was bitterly angry about this, but I reasoned that if the Bible was not true (and I had already made up my mind that it was not), then Christianity was false, since the Bible is its foundation.

Desperate for friends, I eagerly welcomed attention of any type. One day I was sitting in the student lounge when an attractive young woman came up to me and started talking. Her name was Jenny Griffith. There was a hook to the conversation, however. Jenny was a Christian, and she invited me to church. I did not relish the prospect, but I definitely liked the idea of seeing more of Jenny, so I went. Was I in for a shock! This was not like anything I had imagined, for my idea of church was based on very formal, proper, incense-burning Anglican parishes. This church was not like that at all. It was very small, and it had no organ. There were seats instead of pews. The congregation sang lively, upbeat songs and sounded as if they actually enjoyed being there. Everyone was very friendly. Surprisingly, I liked it. This was definitely unlike any other type of church or religious organization I had ever encountered.

I continued returning to this small, friendly, informal little church—although not for the right reasons. I was hoping there might be the possibility of a relationship springing up between Jenny and me. The Lord, meanwhile, had other more significant things in mind, beginning with my salvation!

The Gospel Hits Home

Following one Sunday night service, the pastor of the little church approached me and asked if I wanted to do anything "about it." I asked him what "it" was, and he again responded by asking if I wanted to do anything "about it." I told him I was not interested in "it," and that, for the moment, was the end of the conversation. It was not until later that I learned Pastor Phillip Powell was really asking me if I wanted to commit my life to Jesus Christ. He did not want to be overly pushy and force the situation, hence the mystery about "it." He felt if he came on too strong it might cause me to run out the door and never come back.

As the weeks went on, I continued attending church, and I even started listening to contemporary Christian music at home. I was also developing an interest in what the pastor was saying. It seemed the Lord's hook had caught another fish, and it was time to reel it in. While initially attending church to spend more time with Jenny rather than to learn about Jesus, as I heard the Word preached and taught, it now began to take effect.

One day I purchased a copy of *Good News for Modern Man*, a modern translation of the Bible. For the first time, I read Scripture with an open mind. Instead of considering myself to be so intellectually superior that the Bible had nothing to teach me, I read it with a sincere interest in knowing what it said about who God is. I picked up that book and said, "God, if you're real, please speak to me in a way I can understand." At that point, I can honestly say that I had a genuine, supernatural experience. The letters on the Bible page in front of me appeared to be about six feet tall. From that point on, I read Scripture with a different set of eyes: the eyes of understanding that God gave me. And I knew what I read was true. I asked God to intervene in my life in a way I could grasp, and he honored my request. He will do the same for anyone who asks him.

The Word of God says that "if from there you seek the Lord your God, you will find him if you look for him with all your heart and with all your soul" (Deut. 4:29). That happened to me over thirty years ago, and it was a supernatural experience, a one-of-a-kind encounter where God met me where I was at that time in my life. Although I have had other supernatural experiences, nothing quite like that one has occurred since. That was the coup de grâce. My relationship with the Lord has deepened over the years, and he has communicated with me in many different ways—but nothing quite so dramatically as that time.

Despite that extraordinary incident, I was still not on board with trusting Jesus as my Savior. I had not completely surrendered my life to his control, but the Lord was supernaturally preparing my heart to do so. I did not even know how to "get saved." A week later, however, I was reading a book by an Anglican clergyman named David Watson. He made a very simple yet profoundly compelling statement to the effect that if you have never asked Jesus Christ to be your Lord and Savior, you are not a Christian, and you will be eternally lost.

My newfound understanding of the truth of the Bible swept away any reasons to hesitate. At that moment, I bowed my head and asked Jesus Christ to be the Lord of my life. There were no flashing lights and no further supernatural experiences, only a quiet act of obedience to God's Word. At that point, the future direction of my life became clearer. I was a Christian, and God was beginning an exciting work in me, preparing me for something I could hardly imagine.

Becoming a Christian brought with it certain profound changes in my personality and behavior. My mother began noticing those transformations in me and became rather worried about my sudden religious "fanaticism." She was not overly concerned about the changes she saw at first, because she thought it was just another phase I was going through and that I would get over it. But as my faith solidified and began increasing rather than dissipating, she became very concerned indeed. She even went so far as to make an appointment for me with a local Anglican parish priest. He asked me if I really thought that anyone who did not receive Jesus Christ as his Lord and Savior would go to hell. Assuring him that I most definitely believed just that, he terminated the interview, shaking his head in absolute disbelief. He thought there was no hope for me, but I had an eternal hope by the name of Jesus.

Bible School

I felt the need to receive some Bible college instruction, so I spent the 1976–1977 academic year at a Bible college in South Wales. It was a good experience for the most part, like being in a spiritual hothouse. After finishing that year, I returned home to Bournemouth, where the burning question became what I planned to do with my life. As I prayed, I began to feel God might be calling me to full-time ministry. That was a challenge for me then. The church in England where I met Christ did not give young people the opportunity to make their own decisions about obeying God's calling in their lives. In other words, you were not encouraged to decide individually to obey God. Instead, someone who had more spiritual authority had to decide for you. Still, I followed the call as I heard it by applying to a couple of universities as well as to London Bible College.

I was accepted at LBC, but shortly thereafter I sensed a call from God to go to the United States. I applied to Southeastern College in Lakeland, Florida, and was initially accepted, but that was only the beginning. There were still lots of other issues to be worked out, such as how I planned to pay for everything. While England was very generous in student financial aid, that generosity only extended to those attending British colleges and universities. The British government was not willing to finance a student going to school in the United States. This meant I was at a standstill, unemployed, with an acceptance to an American college valid only if I could come up with the funds to get there and subsequently support myself.

Meanwhile, things were a little rocky at church youth group meetings, where I soon became the object of humor—especially when there were guest speakers. When other young people introduced themselves to guests and said what they did for a living, they would laughingly say, "Oh, that's Jeremy Reynalds, and he's going to America!" The months dragged on, and I was not any closer to getting over the pond. Had I missed God's calling in my life? Should I abandon the entire plan?

I was on the verge of giving up my idea to immigrate to the United States when, a few weeks later, something very interesting happened. I had been corresponding with a minister who had previously spent some time in the United States, and he invited me to meet him. Consequently, a few weeks later, I took the train from Bournemouth to London, a journey of about one hundred miles, to meet with this individual. I told him all my woes, hoping he might offer me some money. He did not. Instead, he told me, "Jeremy, you say that God has called you to America. But right now you have a lot of time on your hands. I wish I had the amount of time you do. Go home and make up your mind that you are going. If you say God has told you, then act on it." This man's sound advice caused a change in my thinking. God used his words to speak deeply to my heart, and I knew from then on that I would be crossing the pond to America.

America, Here I Come!

Three days after meeting with the minister in London, a lady asked me how my plans to go to the United States were going. She did not profess any relationship with Christ, but I knew her through some friends. After I told her I was going no matter what, she gave me two hundred dollars for the airfare. Ten days later I was offered a place to stay in Orlando, Florida, by an English pastor and his wife, who opened their home to me without even knowing who I was.

I was on the plane two weeks after this. Even though I was actually flying across the Atlantic, it was still hard for me to believe that what I had dreamed of, hoped for, and prayed about for so long was becoming a reality. What was in store? I might not have been so keen to go had I known. In time, what awaited me was poverty, homelessness, almost losing my ministry, and an eventual divorce. All that and more came later, but one thing I learned right off the bat was that it was time for me to grow up. I was on my own now. For the previous twenty years, I had lived a relatively pampered life with a guaranteed roof over my head and three meals a day. Whether I worked really made no difference. Now things had changed, and it was just the Lord and me. I knew I would have to take care of myself.

Just before I left for the States, my mother said I was making my bed and would have to lie in it, meaning I would face all the consequences of choosing to leave England. She made it quite clear there would be no help from her at all. She had done enough, and now, she said, I was denigrating all her assistance by going to the Colonies (as she dubbed the United States) on a "wild-goose chase." And it was all because of that "fanatical religion."

She did have some reason for the way she felt. My mother had taken wonderful care of both my older brother, Tony, and me. We both benefited from her tutelage and strong English private school educations. Mom felt she had prepared us properly, and I admit I was less than gracious and wise in my comments to her since my conversion. For example, one morning we were in a heated argument. I told this good, upright, caring Englishwoman that she was both a heathen and a sinner! Now, from a scriptural point of view, this was perhaps true. But saying so, and saying so in the way I did, was unkind and unwise. To my mother, a sinner was someone like a prostitute, and a heathen was a half-naked person running around a jungle. To put the matter delicately, my newfound Christian zeal needed some refining! Thankfully, God worked in me to develop the wisdom and compassion I lacked.

I can look back now and see that some of the experiences ahead of me were the Lord's way of preparing me for my work of ministering to the poor and needy. How wonderful God is to weave into our lives the very circumstances he will use to enable us to serve him.

I arrived at Miami International Airport clutching my one-way ticket to America carrying my last fifty dollars in my pocket. At that time in 1978 an Air Florida ticket from Miami to Orlando only cost twenty dollars. Haven't times changed! I was in the United States with thirty dollars in my pocket, and this represented all my worldly wealth.

I disembarked from the plane and made my way to immigration. There were numerous booths from which I could choose, so I prayed and made my selection. I knew I needed to trust God on this and all things, although I did not always do so—to my detriment. The official at the booth asked me what I planned to do while I was in the United

States and how long I wanted to stay. When I told him I wanted to preach the gospel, he looked a little concerned and asked, "Oh, are you going to make a living at that? There are people who make a lot of money doing that." I don't know if he was being cynical or serious. Years later I realized how the Lord had gone before me during that experience when I learned what the official *should* have asked me. He should have asked me if I had a return air ticket to England. If I could not produce one, he should have inquired if I had enough money to purchase one. That would have been protocol. Fortunately for me, he did not ask those things. It seems the Lord was serious about taking a middle-class English boy with absolutely no personal experience of being poor, hungry, and homeless and sending him to the United States to help care for America's needy.

Finally, I arrived at the pastor's house in Orlando. A lady answered the door, introduced herself as Kathy, and said her husband would be back shortly. She gave me tea (naturally, she was English). When her husband, David, arrived, they questioned me closely about my plans and then said something that chilled me. It impacted me so greatly that I still remember it as clearly today as the day it was spoken. Dave said, "Our faith has gotten us here, and if you want to get anywhere, it's going to have to be your faith that does it. You're not going to sponge off us, okay?" With a mouth that went instantly dry, I gulped a quick response, assuring the couple I would not sponge off them. What else was I going to say? Yet I was now in a foreign country, staying with strangers, and U.S. immigration law prevented me from working while holding a visitor's visa. I had nothing. I was very much like the homeless people I would be helping some years down the road: totally dependent on others for my most basic needs.

Dave and Kathy's reception and attitude was not quite what I had expected, and I was caught up short. All sorts of things flooded through my mind during the next few minutes. Maybe I could go back to England without losing too much face and reapply to London Bible College. Maybe … maybe … maybe. I was still trying to determine just exactly what I had really gotten myself into when the couple said they were really tired and showed me my room. I went to bed.

I lay in bed for a long time that night, thinking and wondering. It was obvious this couple was not going to give me a free ride just because I said God had called me to America. If God really had called me, they wanted to see some proof. The next day I could see more trouble brewing on the horizon when, in an expanded version of what they had already told me, they said, "You say God has called you to America. Well, he has called us as well. You are in our house, which is a tangible example of God providing for us. It has a pool and orange trees, and we have plenty of food in our pantry. If God has called you, he will provide for you as well."

I was getting more fearful by the minute. It is one thing to tell your peers in England that God has called you to another country. It sounds sort of grand, even if they do not believe you. But all the while I was telling them I was still being provided for by my parents. Now, God would have to be my provider. If he did not, starvation or deportation was imminent, and those things were all I could think of.

A couple of days passed before I made my first visit to an American church. While I did not know it, sitting in that service was my future wife. But that was not the thing I remember about the service—in fact, I don't even remember seeing her at the time. Neither was the thing I remembered from that first service the sermon or the church building. As odd as it may seem, it was learning that the church had a secretary. This was my first real sense that I was being exposed to the American church culture, and it was a shock. All the evangelical churches I had visited while in England were small and poor. In one, the church did not even have an office for the pastor, who worked out of his house. Even small churches in this new country had secretaries, and to me this seemed an extravagance.

A Different Side of the US

A few days later, Dave and Kathy recommended what they thought was a wonderful idea to introduce me firsthand to the realities of American life. They suggested that I spend the summer with a high-spirited group of Christians who traveled the United States holding tent revivals. This seemed a very unusual and interesting thing to do for a proper English lad. I packed my suitcase and met with a group of other believers from the Orlando area who were planning to spend their summer in the same way. We arrived in Anderson, South Carolina, at about one o'clock in the morning while everyone was asleep—in tents.

This was my introduction to a new way of living. We had long Bible studies in the morning and ate peanut butter and jelly sandwiches, or whatever else was available, for lunch. As a result, to this day I cannot stand peanut butter! In the afternoons, most of us went street witnessing. Following that, we returned to camp, took showers, and had about an hour's free time before participating in long evening revival services. We didn't eat supper until after the evening evangelistic meeting, and by that time, we were pretty much starving. In this thing as well I can now see how the Lord was forming me for my ministry to the needy, which was still some years on the horizon. While in England, I truly never knew what it was like to be poor. I had everything I physically needed, and while I might not have enjoyed every aspect of my upbringing, my experience was still one sought after and envied by many.

England has what is known as council housing. Here in the United States, the equivalent would be the projects. Back in the sixties and seventies, most of this type of housing was painted a uniform drab gray. My image of poor people—their needs, hopes, and problems—was shaped by listening to my mother make derogatory comments about them. She felt that these individuals ended up in project-style housing because of some deficiency in their personality and motivation. She believed, as many did, that the poor could have something better if they only tried harder. The Lord had to straighten out my thinking by leading me gradually into his chosen calling for me. Talk about a strange type of work for God to choose for me. I really cannot think of any more unlikely person to minister to the needs of the poor than myself. My background completely prejudiced me against it.

The Lord did many wonderful things for me my first summer in the United States, especially by giving me many opportunities to share his Word. Many of the circumstances surrounding those events were quite humorous. For example, the evangelist in charge of the young people that first summer was constantly being asked by one visitor to have me preach. After honoring the request a few times, he said to the lady, "You must sure like what Jeremy has to say." "Oh, no," she responded. "I don't understand a word of what he says. I just like his British accent!" God continued showing me the wonders of his provision by supplying my personal needs, as well as those of the group.

At the end of the summer, I returned to Orlando and was invited by Dave and Kathy to stay with them again. Unfortunately, plans for attending the Bible college in Lakeland did not work out, and I really did not know what I was going to do. A few weeks after returning to Orlando, I met Sylvia, my wife-to-be, and we started dating in September of 1978.

I didn't have any money, so we didn't really go out on dates; it was more like a "hanging out" situation. At twenty-one years old, I was still very immature. Sylvia had been married previously and had a child. At the time, she was working full-time in a day care center. I was scarcely on my own and did not have any idea how to support myself, let alone a wife and a family. Nevertheless, a few months later, we were married on April 14, 1979. Sylvia paid for everything, even the rings, because I still could not legally work.

Reality hit me like a hammer following the honeymoon. I was anxious to be in full-time ministry, but I failed to see the Lord's dealings in my life. I was leaning on my own understanding and ability instead of relying on God. Obviously, he knew the significant step I had taken by getting married, and he still had more to teach me. I had also neglected to consider that there could be a significant time difference between receiving the call of God into ministry and being involved in actual ministry. The biblical example of this is when the shepherd David was called to be king of Israel (1 Sam. 16). Although the prophet Samuel anointed him, it was not until some time after that he actually took on the role of king. The waiting time did not invalidate God's calling; it was just God's way of doing things, because there is much to be learned in the waiting.

Those in tune with what the Holy Spirit is saying to them hold that word—that call—in their hearts and know they have special purposes set aside for them to perform in the future. Unfortunately, I was not in harmony with God's timing and wanted to be "God's little helper"—and for him to move along a bit faster! I thought I could help God out by not waiting for his timing. Consequently, I caused a lot of grief for myself and everyone around me. One of the first things I did after marrying Sylvia was apply for my green card, which I subsequently obtained. This meant I could now work. The only problem was I was not trained to do anything in particular. I worked a variety of odd jobs and took some community college courses, all the time wanting to be in full-time ministry. The last thing I wanted to do was wait.

I very foolishly launched myself into a full-time volunteer ministry position. Lack of income resulted in our family becoming homeless in late 1981. A kind family in central Florida agreed to shelter Sylvia, our eight-year-old son, Ben, and our two-and-a-half-year-old son, Joshua. Because of my arrogant attitude, that offer did not extend to me.

On the Road

With my wife and family safe and being provided for, I set out on the road. I had enough money for a bus ticket to Dallas, and from then on my mode of transportation was hitchhiking. On a late, cold evening in January of 1982, I arrived in Dallas. I had about ten dollars in my pocket, and I carried a small suitcase, which seemed unbearably heavy. My thumb had been sticking out in the wind for so long it got frozen and sore and felt like it would drop off. Yet just when I was about to give up, an elderly couple stopped their car. They asked where I was headed. It turned out they were Christians who actually lived their faith, and to me they were like angels sent from heaven. They taught me some incredible lessons. They took me to their home, fed me a delicious meal, gave me a comfortable bed, and took me back to the highway in the morning. Even though it was a dangerous thing for them to do, for me it was a great blessing.

I have found that trials often follow blessings. By the next evening, I had gotten to the New Mexico–Texas border, where I ended up standing out in the blazing sun for hours. As hard as the lessons were to learn, my homeless experiences helped shape the ministry of Joy Junction. For example, I insist that we provide transportation to pick up new residents. I have also instructed my staff to see that guests who come in after the normal arrival time are fed something, no matter what time of the day or night it is.

While I definitely did not enjoy my experience of hunger and homelessness, I know that if I had not gone through them, I would not have appreciated how good a bologna sandwich could taste when you have not eaten for a long time. If that church had not offered me shelter five miles away, I would not have understood how hopelessly distant and unreachable five miles sounds when you are broke, exhausted, and homeless.

Later, I arrived in Phoenix, and friends bought me a bus ticket to Flagstaff, where they picked me up and took me to their home in Cameron, Arizona. For the next few weeks, I stayed in Cameron, a little village on an Indian reservation, about fifty miles north of Flagstaff. I spent a lot of time thinking about my life's direction.

A few weeks later, on a wing and a prayer—really more of a wing than a prayer—I traveled to Santa Fe, New Mexico, the site of a bloody prison riot a year or so earlier. I heard that the penitentiary was hiring prison guards, and the pay was good. I arrived in Santa Fe on a Saturday evening. That night, I stayed in a hotel, and the following morning I made my way to Christian Life Fellowship, at that time pastored by Carl Conley. He not only became my pastor but also remained a good friend throughout the years.

Another fortuitous event was about to happen. Following the service, a church member offered me a place to stay for a week, and afterward I stayed in the basement of another church member, a local property owner named Rudy Rodriguez. Rudy put me to work painting apartments for him, which must have required continuing faith and patience on his part, as I ended up spilling more paint on the floors than I put on the walls. Consequently, even long-suffering Rudy decided it would be best if I looked for another job.

A local hotel hired me, and I worked there for a while, washing dishes and driving their van. During this time, Rudy and the members of the Santa Fe chapter of the Full Gospel Businessmen's Fellowship collected money for me to bring Sylvia and our boys from Florida to Santa Fe. By this time, she was about eight months pregnant.

Sylvia arrived a few weeks later. New Mexico provided a big climate change and a culture shock after living in Florida. While it was good having a job and a roof over our heads, it was not easy living on minimum wage in Santa Fe. Still, we were more blessed than many Americans.

Thirty-plus years later, Rudy still helps us. What a blessing he is.

Faltering First Steps

Change was in the air again. My boss came to me one day and said that the owner of the hotel had just paid a visit and had decided to make some staff reductions. I was one of those included in the reduction. Sylvia was less than thrilled when I arrived home and told her that I had been laid off. No job meant no money, and that could mean being homeless again.

Before the layoff, however, one of the managers approached me and said he thought it was a blessing that I had lost my job. Seeing my look of amazement, he explained that he felt the Lord was opening the way for me to go into full-time ministry. I was not really enthusiastic about this, thinking how easy it was for him to say this to me since he was still employed. I had a growing family, including a brand-new baby, and no job.

Still, I quickly began reflecting about God's call on my life and wondered if this was indeed the time for me to go into full-time service for the Lord. But with what? Definitely not my good looks! I started thinking about a coffeehouse-type of ministry where I could preach the gospel. I started looking for a building. While walking around Santa Fe one day, I ended up in an older section of town on Agua Fria. I found a strip mall composed of three bright pink buildings. One was a barbershop, and the second was a doctor's office. The store that interested me the most, however, was closed and dark and had windows with holes stuffed full of newspapers to fill the cracks.

I went into the barbershop to see what I could find out. The barber told me that while the empty building was rented, it was only used a couple of days a week. The barber gave me the tenant's phone number.

The next week, I went with Pastor Carl Conley to meet this individual, who ran some sort of a private club on weekends. He agreed to sublet to us, and, thinking he was being very helpful, he said that if the project did not work out, it was all right; we could stop leasing any time we wanted. While I was appreciative of the man's kindness, there was no question in my mind that it would work. It had to.

His Place started as a coffeehouse, at first open only a few hours each evening. I did not really know at that time the specifics of what would occur there, other than that I wanted to tell people about Jesus. My prayer was quickly granted, but not quite in the way I had envisioned. One night I sat alone in His Place for hours before anyone came by. At about nine thirty at night, a truck stopped by, and I heard some men saying to someone outside, "Go in there. You're wasted. Get some coffee and sober up before you go home to the old lady." For the next couple of hours, I had a captive, albeit drunk, audience to tell about Jesus.

My work at the coffeehouse gave me a taste for ministry, and I began enjoying it. We had potluck suppers every Tuesday, and for a while, it was almost as if we were the only Christian revival center in Santa Fe. When word spread we were giving away free food, that was all she wrote, and the poor, needy, and homeless started coming in. I didn't go out to try and find them—they just found me. Tragically, though, as fast as the homeless started appearing, the Christians who had been coming for the teaching and music ministry started leaving.

As the months sped by, I decided I would really like to turn His Place into an overnight shelter. But there was a problem. With the main tenant occupying the facility for a couple of evenings a week, it just was not possible. So I prayed, asked for the Lord's help, and for once in my life, left things in his hands.

A Learning Time

When the main tenant moved, we eventually opened up as an overnight shelter, offering beds to homeless men. Back in those days, I was still very naive in thinking that if you gave homeless people a place to stay and a meal, they would automatically be grateful. It never occurred to me that people might not be thankful for something free, and that they might even take advantage of you. But my first phone bill showed that there were some homeless people who would not think twice about using you. That was my crash course in running a shelter.

As the months and years went on, His Place gradually assumed more and more responsibility for taking care of Santa Fe's homeless. The daily *Santa Fe New Mexican* published a wonderfully descriptive article about the shelter written in the mid-1980s by freelance writer Douglas Conwell.

> The aim of His Place Coffeehouse is more than physical fare. It also includes spiritual fare. The "His" is Jesus, and the message is that "He" can change lives and give hope to the lost and forlorn. Today, the bright pink building on Agua Fria Street is more than a coffeehouse, although that is how it got its start in July 1982. Now it is a residential shelter for eight men, with a companion women's residence nearby—one of the few resources of its kind in northern New Mexico.
>
> His Place was the idea of a transplanted Englishman named Jeremy Reynalds, who heard the "call of the Lord" to come to America. Reynalds arrived in Orlando, Florida, in 1978, with $50 in his pocket and a sense of mission in his heart. He worked a number of odd jobs, married, and then moved in with his wife, just cruising about looking for some place to happen.
>
> It happened in Santa Fe, where he was offered a place to live and found employment. It didn't take him long to recognize a "desperate need" for services to the homeless; but he also recognized that as a relative newcomer, there was also a need to establish his own credibility.
>
> Within a short six months, however, Reynalds was serving the ministry of his church, Christian Life Fellowship, through the ministry of the coffeehouse. Reynalds credits the help of several people, including Blackie Gonzales, president of KCHF-TV in Santa Fe, and owner of KDAZ Radio in

Albuquerque. Gonzales offered Reynalds half a day's free air time on radio and all the income he could earn from selling advertising spots. Enthusiastic conviction made him a successful salesman. Meanwhile, moral (and later financial) support came from Pastor Carl Conley of Christian Life Fellowship.

First only open for a few hours a day for coffee and doughnuts, His Place remodeled and opened as a shelter for homeless men in November 1983. A similar sized women's residence opened recently. Together, they accept a large number of referrals from police, social services, churches, mental health centers as well as city and state offices. And with at least somewhere for the homeless to go, the possibility of their causing trouble is reduced. As Reynalds said, "Somebody cold and hungry is more likely to steal than somebody well fed."

Not just the homeless come to His Place. There are some area families who are faced with the choice of either eating or paying the rent. They come to His Place so they do not have to make that terrible decision. As Reynalds said, "We help anyone we can in any way we can. We figure if we're going to be in the neighborhood, we'd like to help out."

Being neighborly has been a priority, as some of the nearby residents were not sure about the location of a shelter in their area. Reynalds makes a special effort to communicate and cooperate with these neighbors, and keep the area clean and well organized.

His Place does much more than just feed and house people. Of course imparting the message of Jesus Christ is foremost, and residents are required to attend regular devotional services and other events. But religion is seen in context with a person's life in the community and the feeling of self-worth.

Reynalds said that His Place aims to "provide an uplifting atmosphere and to let people know the shelter staff loves and cares for them. Our whole aim is to make people responsible. We help them through a transition from feeling broken down, useless and feeling incapable of feeding themselves or working, to being a person who can put a few bucks away and put a down payment on an apartment."

All residents are expected to find work, but Reynalds tells them, "Hey, I don't expect you to work harder than I do." There is little chance of that—as Reynalds puts in sometimes more than 60 hours a week.

The hundreds who come to the door on Agua Fria have gone through many doors before—doors of divorce, broken homes, alcoholism and drug addiction and aimless wandering from halfway house to rescue mission. Many are in a cycle of poverty, dependent on public assistance that does not meet living expenses but is enough money not to give up. Frequently they have been told they are worthless; and most have come to believe it.

The coffeehouse tries to break that cycle with the force of love, but also with rigidly enforced structure. Each person must search daily for employment. "This is not a flop house," Reynalds emphasized. There are plenty of other places for people to flop.

Although the maximum stay is 14 days, Reynalds is flexible. If someone fails to try and improve their situation, they are asked to leave. On the other hand, if a person is making a genuine effort to succeed and just has not had any luck finding a place to stay, then he or she is allowed to stay longer.

Conwell really captured our reasons for existing, and his article was a great source of encouragement to me. His Place provided a training ground and cemented God's calling on my life to minister to the homeless. But in almost four years of running the shelter, I had taken only four days off. In February of 1986, Sylvia and I took a couple of days rest in Phoenix. During that time, I felt God speaking to me about resigning from my position at His Place, which I did, effective May 31, 1986. Unfortunately, I made a major mistake when I told the Lord I would do whatever he wanted—except that I would never run a shelter again. Never tell the Lord never!

The month of May came very quickly. I looked at the possibility of pastoring a church, but there were no churches available. My replacement for His Place arrived and expected me to be moving on quickly.

The "Almost Homeless" Former Shelter Operator

By this time I was really desperate and needed a place for our family to stay, as our house went with the job. How ironic that the home giver was about to become homeless!

I called a longtime friend who lived in Taos, New Mexico, sixty-five miles north of where we were living, and he offered us a place to stay. The experience tested the friendship of both families, but we all survived the experience, and that friend is now on the board of directors for Joy Junction.

I tried finding employment, but after a few weeks there were still no job offers. I was getting worried and began sinking into depression. While living in Santa Fe, I had made brief contact with an individual running a shelter located on Kirtland Air Force Base. The ministry was called the Reach Out to Jesus Family Chapel, and it was part of a program initiated by the Department of Defense. The program allowed nonprofit corporations to use vacant military buildings to help the homeless. The director of the program invited me to help him.

We stayed for a few weeks, but I knew God had something else for me to do. One morning while praying and considering my future, the Lord called to my mind a vacant property in Albuquerque's South Valley. All I knew about the acreage was that it was large and had formerly been used by an area alcohol and drug rehabilitation program operated by Christians. It had been vacant for some months following the closure of the program.

I went down one morning to check out the property, and I was impressed with what I saw. I contacted the board president of the group that owned the property and told him I wanted to open a shelter for homeless families, using the available land and buildings. He said he would get back to me. I really was not expecting him or the other board members to take me seriously, but what I didn't know was that prior to my application, several board members had been thinking that a homeless shelter would be a good use for this property. Isn't it amazing how God had given me favor with these men before I even approached them? This is exactly how he works.

A New Home

During the period between His Place and where I was now, God dealt with my heart by showing me in a variety of ways that he still wanted me to house and feed homeless and hungry people. However much I might not have chosen that calling for myself, it was clear this is what God wanted me to do.

A few weeks later, I received a call from the property owners telling me that the board members had accepted my proposal. I was ecstatic! The terms were reasonable, including a week's free rent on a mobile home for my family and five weeks free rent on a ministry building for the homeless. After that, the rent would be $650 a month. While that was not a lot of money, back then it seemed like a fortune. Anything is a great deal when you have next to nothing. But I have always thought the word *poor* can be a relative term. One can be materially poor and spiritually wealthy, or vice versa.

In any event, we moved onto the property, which I decided to call Joy Junction. I was extremely grateful we all had a home again. The trailer was not much, but it was home, and we didn't have to share it with anyone. I rapidly became busy. Looking back, I can see several indications God's hand was on the shelter right from the beginning. First, I began the work because I believed it was God's calling on my life. Second, the timing was right. Shortly after I left the shelter on Kirtland Air Force Base, it closed. A small shelter for families run by another local agency also closed, making Joy Junction the only family shelter in the entire Albuquerque area.

The Joy Junction ministry grew rapidly, and so did the income. Shelter income climbed from $11,000 the first year to about $300,000 in 1990. The Lord blessed my efforts, and the shelter quickly gained a good reputation. Joy Junction was often featured in positive stories on local television newscasts and in local newspaper articles. My God-given skill was definitely in the production of publicity to get attention for the ministry.

Although I had previously done everything from keeping the books to teaching many of the regular evening Bible studies, the day-to-day financial management of the shelter began to escape me and those I had entrusted with the accounting. While I knew the shelter was struggling financially, I did not know what to do about it. There were outstanding bills and staff salaries that could not be paid, and I saw no way to get out of the financial hole into which I was all too rapidly sinking.

Crisis!

The pressure quickly mounted, so much so that I felt I just could not take it anymore. I decided the only solution was to go public with the problems the shelter was facing. I announced a public ultimatum that if at least $20,000 was not raised by the end of the next month, I would close Joy Junction. This was not necessarily the best thing to do, but at the time I was absolutely desperate and could not see any other way. I felt totally on my own and did not even know whom to ask for help. Various local television and radio stations publicized the need, and some additional finances started to come in. I thought perhaps things were beginning to look up, but in reality I had not even seen the beginning of where things were headed. A lot of troubles, trials, and trauma lay just a few weeks ahead.

A reporter from the *Albuquerque Journal*, Leah Lorber, called and wanted to do an in-depth story. It became apparent she did not want to do a light, fluffy report detailing the shelter's need, but rather a hard-nosed investigative piece about the problems we were having. It turned out to be the most frightening ordeal of my life.

The next week I spent long hours with Leah. She was going to tell the community why the shelter was in its financial bind, and I was going to be held accountable for everything that had happened. She wanted to see a budget to help explain how we got in such dire financial straits. Now, budgets were foreign to me. I had been so busy raising money to pay bills, answering telephones, signing in homeless people, and running the shelter that the idea of a budget never even occurred to me. Obviously, I had a lot to learn about the financial aspects of running a shelter.

I want to say clearly that while I had the best of intentions, so the road to hell is paved (yes, that old expression is true). And good intentions just do not cut it when you are dealing with the public's money. You have to know what is expected of you. At that point, I honestly did not know. Not even close. I was naive in more ways than one.

The reporter concluded her first session by asking me if I had copies of the shelter's 990, an Internal Revenue Service form that nonprofit organizations are required to submit each year to the IRS. I referred her to the shelter's volunteer bookkeeper, never dreaming what the result might be. A few days later, Leah called me to request a second interview. The questions went something like this: "Jeremy, can you tell me about the bounced checks and the unpaid payroll taxes for the shelter?" My heart sank. How did she know? The volunteer accountant had told her. After all, I never told him he should not, and my sending the reporter to see him made him think he was to answer any question he was asked.

I decided there was only one thing to do. As the reporter continued to reel though a list of problem areas, I looked her right in the eyes and said, "Leah, the public is tired of hearing excuses and seeing the blame put on someone else. As head of Joy Junction, I take the blame. Many of our problems and inefficiencies are due to an excessive workload on my part and an organization that has grown incredibly fast—maybe too fast."

During the next few days, Leah contacted me numerous times and added details to her story. Needless to say, I was growing increasingly apprehensive about exactly how the story would be presented. I rushed to get the newspaper each morning, wondering if that edition of the paper was going to be one where the story would appear. One Saturday morning, I ran to get the paper and hastily opened it up. The story was worse than I thought. There, right at the top of the main section (above the fold), was a long article headlined "Joy Junction Runs by Seat of the Pants Finances." To add insult to injury, the paper used the worst picture of me I had ever seen.

After letting the article sink in, I dragged myself to the office. The phone started ringing. Some of the callers said they were disgusted and angry. But many calls were supportive. One summed up several others: "You've done too much for too many with too little for too long. It's time we came forward and helped you."

The *Albuquerque Journal* article showed me many things. Some people I believed were real friends completely ignored me after that. Then there were those I never thought even cared for the ministry who came forward and offered prayer and financial support. One of those who stuck with me through everything and encouraged me during this difficult time was Gino Geraci, then an associate pastor of Calvary of Albuquerque and now the pastor of Calvary South Denver. Carl Conley also made himself available to me immediately, as he had for many years, and agreed to step in for as long as I needed him. He also served as board president for a while.

Many people told me afterward that the reason they continued to support the shelter was because I admitted full responsibility. While some of the things for which I was blamed were not directly attributable to me, in a real sense they were, because I was the leader of the ministry.

Months later, when the same reporter interviewed me again, she said she believed me because I had not attempted to hide anything from her. I was open in all my answers to her very probing questions. There was never any hint of financial impropriety or questionable actions. As I said before, the main problem was being overburdened and too busy to oversee everything effectively.

According to Romans 8:28, the Lord turns everything to the good if we let him. The apostle Paul said, "And we know that in all things God works for the good of those who love him, who have been called according to his purpose." That has certainly been proven true in my life and the work of Joy Junction.

The result of Leah's article was the expansion of our ministry board and the Lord's gift of a business manager, something I had needed for a long time. The *Albuquerque Journal* later put it like this: "Joy Junction has bowed to the inevitable, and put its financial affairs under the watchful eyes of a business manager." For a while, I joked with our new business manager, calling him "the inevitable."

One vision yet to be fulfilled was the purchase of our fifty-two-acre property in Albuquerque's South Valley. That blessing would come soon enough.

The Promised Land

The Old Testament tells the story about how the patriarchs traveled through the wilderness to find the Promised Land. From the very beginning of Joy Junction in 1986, the Lord gave me a vision to claim that land in the name of Christ for the homeless of Albuquerque.

Most of the other agencies and ministries in Albuquerque that deal with the homeless are downtown. They have absolutely no room to grow, and even when a possible opportunity presents itself, angry neighbors predictably rise in a chorus of protest against any expansion. We are in a somewhat different situation because Joy Junction's nearest neighbor immediately to the north is the city of Albuquerque's sewage treatment plant. One day, while speaking to the director of that facility, I told him that our two agencies really had a lot in common. A little surprised, he asked why I believed that to be so. I told him that while everyone was in agreement that we both provided important services for the city, nobody wanted either one of us as their next-door neighbor!

During the last few years, there has arisen an increasingly hostile climate to the homeless in downtown Albuquerque. Proponents of downtown revitalization have felt that for the downtown district to become an area where people want to spend their time, the homeless have to leave. Some years ago, members of a group of individuals and businesses attempting to revamp Albuquerque's jaded downtown image handed out a report filled with recommendations on dealing with the "problem" of the area's homeless population.

Sadly, the homeless were no longer people to be helped—human beings with souls, minds, and bodies. Instead, they were considered a problem that was standing in the way of business and needed to be moved out of the downtown area. No one quite knew where the homeless could be relocated. The only thing the neighborhood association spokespersons could tell the area media was that the homeless should not be moved into their area. How deplorable. Tragically, the situation hasn't gotten that much better.

Buying the Land

With this sort of attitude gaining ground in our area, it became important for us to secure our fifty-two-acre property. Let me explain what that entailed. While our landlords had generously offered to donate ten acres to us, we would have to pay the appraised price of $19,000 per acre if we wanted more. We eventually managed to buy the remaining forty-two acres, where, in addition to housing the needy, we grow crops. I am unable to report any dazzling overnight miracles concerning the purchase of this acreage, such as a huge sum of money given to us at the eleventh hour that enabled us to buy the property without going into debt. Rather, it took us a long time to come to the place where we could buy that additional forty-two acres, and the process involved a lot of prayer and a capital campaign of sorts. Fundraising for capital projects is always difficult, and I pray that this account of how the Lord dealt with us will encourage you.

Having been involved in ministry to the homeless for over thirty years, I have studied quite a lot of material about capital campaigns. Most of what one hears about capital fund drives run by agencies specializing in raising money suggests that they are all overwhelmingly successful. Maybe that is because they cost such a huge amount of money to finance. I remember one quote we got from an agency to undertake a capital campaign for Joy Junction was for almost $100,000. This seemed to be a classic case of where, in order to raise money, you had to already have money. Where were we going to get $100,000? My thinking was that if we could get ahold of that sort of money, we probably would not need to have a capital campaign in the first place. In any event, not having the money, we mostly went it alone.

With some help from a friend of the shelter, we came up with a nicely designed appeal letter to our donors, announcing our desire to purchase the property. Despite that letter, on which we pinned all our hopes, we soon realized we had a problem. Although we prayed fervently, money for the capital campaign was not coming in nearly as fast as or in the amount we needed. Therefore, we initially resigned ourselves to settling for the ten free acres our landlords were willing to donate. Of course, I really should have been much more grateful. That ten-acre property donation from our landlords was a great gift and blessing.

Even though the additional funds we needed were not coming in, our landlords (another Christian ministry) told us to be encouraged and said they really believed in what we were doing. They said their donation was prompted by a desire to ensure our successful continuance should we not be able to either raise enough money or convince a bank to give us a loan to secure the rest of the acreage.

We found a Texas-based company that specialized in church bonds to raise money for property acquisition. After reviewing our financial statements, company representatives said they would like to work with us on a program to allow us to buy about twenty-one of the available forty-two acres. A company representative came out to Albuquerque, and we had a series of meetings to try to generate enough interest in the program. After three such meetings, it looked like we had succeeded in our goal.

The Lord, however, who always has an incredible plan as well as a wonderful sense of humor, had something else in mind. I am unable to tell the story any better than *Albuquerque Journal* reporter Paul Logan in a September 1996 story. Here is his account:

> Joy Junction has scrapped plans to sell $330,000 in general obligation bonds and will use a bank loan to buy the land it leases.
> The Albuquerque homeless shelter and Bank of New Mexico have signed a letter of commitment for a 15-year mortgage on the 25-acre property and buildings at 4500

> Second Street, shelter executive director Jeremy Reynalds said Friday.
>
> The bank became interested in loaning the money to Joy Junction after learning about the shelter's plan to hold a public bond offering, Reynalds said. Great Nation Investment Corp., a Texas investment-banking firm, had been working with the shelter on the bond deal.
>
> A Great Nation representative contacted Bank of New Mexico about investing in the bond deal, banker Steven Scholl said Friday. The bank decided not to invest, but Scholl said he told the representative the bank was "interested from a loan standpoint."
>
> Great Nation passed along Bank of New Mexico's proposal to the shelter. Joy Junction's board decided last week to take the bank up on its offer instead of selling the bonds, Reynalds said.
>
> "By giving us the tip," he said of Great Nation, "they basically did themselves out of business."
>
> Until Bank of New Mexico's interest, Joy Junction and the Amarillo firm were planning to complete the bond deal, Reynalds said.
>
> Earlier this month, Great Nation held three meetings in Albuquerque to answer prospective investors' questions about the bond offering. Reynalds said that about 38 people made bond inquiries and that it was enough investment interest to go ahead with the bond issuance.

Interestingly, by the time everything had been worked out so we could buy the land, our small, locally owned Bank of New Mexico had been acquired by one of the nation's then megabanks—which had turned us down for a property acquisition loan a few years before.

At about ten o'clock the night before we were due to sign the final documents on Labor Day of 1998, my pager vibrated. Recognizing the number on the small screen as that of our landlords, my heart sank. Being a pessimist by nature, I immediately began thinking, *Oh well, I guess we won't buy the property after all. Something's gone wrong.* After all, why else would there be a call at that time of night?

I called the number, and our attorney answered the phone. Rather than telling me the sale was off, he just asked me if it could be postponed a few hours. He and the attorney for our landlords were feverishly working on last-minute paperwork and trying to tie up loose ends. I breathed a big sigh of relief.

I slept restlessly that night, but finally the morning came. The big day had arrived: after more than twelve years of renting property, Joy Junction was going to be a property owner. It was still hard for me to believe. I had prayed and dreamed about this day for so long that I had a hard time convincing myself it was really happening.

Later that day, I excitedly met our business manager and our attorney over at the title company. Representatives for our landlords turned up a little later. After a three-hour marathon of signing more documents at one time than I had ever signed before, it was all over. We now owned thirty-one acres of property! That included the ten acres gifted to us by our landlords and the twenty-one we had purchased. During a break in the process, our attorney gravely reminded us that we were now legally and morally obligated to make a sizable mortgage payment each month. Even though I knew the Lord was faithful to allow us to make that monthly payment for the next fifteen years, I felt he had entrusted us with an awesome responsibility.

Even though I was thrilled that we now owned thirty-one acres, I still had my heart set on the additional twenty-one acres that were still available. And I felt very strongly that the Lord wanted us to buy that acreage.

More Land

I prayed, racked my brains, and sent lots of press releases to the media detailing my concern. And I pleaded with God to make a way for us to buy this additional land. Yet nothing seemed to be happening. For a while, it seemed to me I was the only one who realized (or cared about) the importance of this additional property purchase. My feeling was that unless we purchased the available land quickly, we might never get another opportunity. It would be sold to whoever made an offer, and then, I was convinced, the zoning could be changed to disallow a shelter for the homeless. If someone else bought the property, there would be absolutely no chance of ever seeing the land used for the ministry of Joy Junction.

The bank did not want to lend us any more money. Bank officials indicated they were open to talking more at some time in the future, but we did not have the luxury of waiting that long. Understandably, our landlords felt that they needed to sell the property as soon as possible. If we were able to come up with cash or proof that a bank was willing to grant us a loan, they would be happy to sell us the property. But if not, they reminded me, a "for sale" sign would be posted. I kept on praying.

A few days later, a postcard miraculously arrived from a company offering church bonds, much like the company we had dealt with previously. This company specialized in assisting churches, not ministries such as Joy Junction. Yet after telephone calls and submitting some financial documents, I learned this group was willing to help us with a bond issuance large enough for us to pay back the debt on the twenty-one acres we bought in 1998—as well as allow us to buy the twenty-one additional acres.

What pleased me no end was that the company was willing to sell most of the bonds to its own investors. This meant it would not be necessary for us to conduct public meetings to sell these bonds to our donors, something that, I explained to company officials, I was far from enthusiastic about doing. On the surface of things, this seemed like the answer to our prayers, but as our business manager consistently reminded me in our weekly meetings, the fees this company charged for their services were very expensive. Consequently, we decided to continue looking for other avenues of funding while keeping our options open with this company.

Sometime later, while listening to early morning talk radio, I heard an advertisement for a small local bank that had recently opened in Albuquerque. Since small local banks are usually thought of as being much more approachable and open to community needs than the national chains, I gave them a call.

Much to my excitement, bank officials expressed an initial interest and encouraged us to stay in touch. After sending the officials our audits and other financial data, two of the bank's officers came down to visit the property. The visit appeared to go smoothly, and I remained quite optimistic that this institution would be willing to provide sufficient financing for us not only to buy the additional acreage we wanted but also to refinance (at a better rate) the property we had already purchased and financed through the other bank. Everything went just as planned, with no last-minute disasters or even any hitches. Closing day arrived, and along with our business manager, I found myself back again at the title company, signing lots of documents. Joy Junction was now the proud owner of fifty-two acres of property—and responsible for a $7,400 monthly mortgage payment to the bank.

I was elated, as this acquisition allowed the shelter ministry a sense of permanence and stability that as renters we had never experienced. To me, it also meant an increased hope that however hostile downtown business owners grew toward the homeless, and however large the homeless population grew in Albuquerque, we would be able, with the Lord's help, to be a part of the solution.

Renovation

Now that we owned the property, our next step was renovation, which we could do only as funds became available. On the fifty-two acres sits a beautiful but dilapidated adobe chapel. For a number of reasons, it had fallen into disrepair over the thirteen years Joy Junction occupied the other part of the property. Since we are a faith-based ministry, I felt it was important for us to make a statement about what was most important to us. With that in mind, I thought it would be appropriate to renovate the chapel first. At least those were my plans then. How our plans do change!

Let me tell you how the chapel came to be in such a neglected state. I woke up one morning in early 1987 and discovered that the entire chapel basement, which was about six feet high, was flooded. The property owners at the time bought a water pump and pumped out the basement, but mixing water with adobe can quickly result in disaster. The chapel was no exception, and that flood nearly became the straw that broke the camel's back. The building already suffered from structural problems, and the water damage, combined with the lack of use, eventually reduced it to a shadow of its former self. But help was on the way in the form of Robert Crawford, a former Joy Junction chaplain.

One day, shortly after buying the first twenty-one acres of our property, I was discussing with one of my staff members what we could do to draw attention to the sad plight of the chapel. Without ever thinking he would agree, we came up with the idea of asking our chaplain if he would consider living on the roof of the chapel for a while. To our amazement, he agreed! We sent out press releases describing the plan. That was the beginning of a torrent of publicity documenting Robert Crawford's forty-day-plus rooftop spiritual experience.

What was interesting to me was that this was not the first time I had attempted bringing the plight of the chapel to the attention of the media, but it was the first time I had personalized it. A few weeks prior to this, I had sent a release to Albuquerque media outlets describing the sad condition of a "possibly historic" building. One local television station had responded, but that was it. Nobody else appeared to be interested. But what a difference we saw when we put a living, breathing person on the chapel roof! Here is what one reporter wrote in the *Albuquerque Journal*:

> On the grounds of Joy Junction, Albuquerque's largest emergency homeless shelter, sits the former, and now derelict, Our Lady of Lourdes Chapel. In an attempt to raise public awareness about the need for restoration of this once beautiful building, Joy Junction Chaplain Robert Crawford is forsaking a warm bed and the comforts of home to live on the chapel roof. With Crawford's "home away-from home," a tent, already in place, and a "port-a-john" at the base of the chapel (insurance regulations prevented the "port-a-john" from being hoisted onto the roof), Crawford has begun his adventure.
>
> Shelter director Jeremy Reynalds said he admires Crawford's

commitment to seeing the chapel renovated. "Judging from comments I've heard here and there over the past decade, this chapel holds a lot of memories for quite a number of people. It's a beautiful building, possibly historically significant, and we'd like to see it restored to its former beauty. It would be a wonderful place to have services for our guests and also to hold some of our community events," said Reynalds.

Reynalds said that Crawford has told him that he plans to stay on the roof until enough funds have been raised for restoration.

"And that—very conservatively speaking—will be at least $100,000, and that's with a lot of volunteer labor," Reynalds added.

In addition to funds for the chapel renovation, Reynalds said that Crawford is open to donations of home cooked meals, hot cocoa and anything to help pass his time of "exile."

Crawford's wife has declined an offer by her husband to join him in this exciting adventure, saying that there'll be no fighting over the television remote while she and her husband are apart.

The media attention continued. In addition to coverage in the *Journal*, Crawford soon became quite familiar with reporters and photographers from the local CBS, ABC, and NBC affiliates. I am sure they provided some welcome relief from the monotony he experienced while spending so many hours, days, and weeks away from his wife and the comforts of home.

Although Crawford planned to stay on the chapel roof until all the necessary funds were raised to renovate the chapel, the Lord had other plans. He cut short his ambitious plans because he had to leave Joy Junction to go to Missouri and help care for his ailing father. By the end of his rooftop stay, he had raised about $11,000.

Even though we raised only 10 percent of our total goal, the project was not a failure. While I was admittedly disappointed about not reaching the $100,000 mark, I look back at the project as a success—just not the sort of success I had originally envisioned. Why? Because we were able to bring the need of the chapel's restoration to a large number of Albuquerqueans, and out of the efforts of the "rooftop reverend," we had for a while some excellent help in restoring the Our Lady of Lourdes Chapel. Alas, community interest and funding waned, leaving the restoration unfinished. We were, however, able to gather enough interest to do some structural work to keep the chapel from incurring any further damage.

I was poignantly reminded one day that the chapel holds many memories for people in the Albuquerque community. One quiet Sunday afternoon, I saw an elderly couple driving around our property. It turned out that the man had gone to school on our property back in the mid-1930s, when it was a Catholic boy's school. He told me he had helped build the chapel. I asked him if he would like to see the inside, and he quickly accepted. He enthusiastically pointed to some of the beams on the chapel roof and proudly told me that those were the beams he had put up there himself as the chapel was being built. It was evident that just being there brought back myriad boyhood memories. It is events like this that act as a constant reminder of the need to renovate this beautiful old house of worship.

Education for Excellence

My vision for reaching the homeless led to obtaining a bachelor's degree with a focus in journalism and a master's degree in communication from the University of New Mexico. In 2006, after seven years of additional study, I earned a Ph.D. in intercultural education from Biola University in California. The thought of obtaining an undergraduate degree, let alone graduate degrees, was the furthest thing from my mind when I began Joy Junction. After all, I was thirty-three when I began undergraduate studies at UNM, and I had a time-consuming position as director of Joy Junction. Beyond that, I had a wife and five children to care for. Yet I definitely felt the Lord wanted me to refine my skills to do the best possible job for him, and so I embarked on university studies.

I obtained my undergraduate degree in 1996 and a master's degree in 1998. By this time, I was hooked on school and wanted to continue. But a desire to study in a Ph.D. program doesn't always mean you will be able to do so. I was therefore thrilled when I was accepted into the doctoral program in intercultural education at Biola University, located just outside Los Angeles. Although I was busy directing the daily operations at the New Mexico–based ministry of Joy Junction, I also felt God wanted me at Biola. My only option was to commute. One day a week, I flew out to southern California to attend classes. Feeling that this was probably not how the typical shelter director spends his or her time, I thought the local media might be interested in featuring a story on my travels. Consequently, I sent them the following press release:

> Joy Junction Founder and Executive Director Jeremy Reynalds is planning on racking up a lot of frequent flyer miles over the next few years. Reynalds has begun taking classes toward his Ph.D. in intercultural education—at Biola University in Southern California. He's flying to Los Angeles every Thursday afternoon and returning to Albuquerque early Friday morning.
>
> Running New Mexico's largest emergency homeless shelter and doing six hours of classes toward an advanced degree would make some younger folk think twice, but Reynalds has never been one to be put off by a challenge. To finance the cost of four air trips a month to California, Reynalds will be teaching two public speaking classes as a part-time instructor at the University of New Mexico.
>
> Reynalds, 42, who has an undergraduate degree in journalism and a master's degree in communication from the University of New Mexico (in addition to being a published author), says he is looking forward to a new school, even if the schedule threatens to be somewhat punishing. "I'm used to hard work and will be in constant contact with Joy Junction for the few hours I'll be in California. I'm also very excited because my schooling thus far has been of tremendous benefit to the shelter."

This release produced much more attention than I originally anticipated. The *Albuquerque Journal* decided to write a personality profile on me and at the same time try to dispel some rumors started about the shelter and me by a small number of disgruntled former residents. The finished product by *Journal* staff writer Rick Nathanson appeared on Friday, November 12, 1999, and it was headlined with a quote from me: "If hoping to get free news coverage to tell the plight of the homeless is shameless self-promotion, then I stand guilty as charged. In order for us to continue getting funds from the community, our name has to be kept before the public." Appropriately, it concluded with a shelter guest summing up her stay by telling the reporter, "Joy Junction allowed the family to stay together, and that's the most important thing."

From 1999 through 2002, I commuted weekly from Albuquerque to Los Angeles. Believe me, this was some sort of feat for someone desperately afraid of flying! The Lord most definitely has ways of keeping us on our toes. He doesn't want us to be afraid of anything and will deal with us directly in the areas where we are fearful.

The Tide of Time

Two dramatic trips punctuated my weekly trips to Biola, one that touched only my life, and another that touched the whole nation. The first event was the death of my mother in 2000. My wife and then my pastor encouraged me to visit her in late February of 2000, a few weeks before she died. I am so glad I made the trip to England when I did.

When there, I made my way slowly up the stairs to the second floor of the hospital in south England, where my mother was a "guest" of the country's nationalized health service. She was in the geriatric unit, and as I walked through the ward, I passed a number of elderly people in various states of mental and physical decay.

I had been warned that my mother's health was rapidly deteriorating, but I was still shocked when I saw her. She was sleeping, and her breathing was labored. Her hands were badly swollen, and her once immaculately coiffed hair fell untidily in all the wrong places. My mother was not fully aware of her surroundings or who was present.

There was little I could do except express my love. After a second visit, I returned to New Mexico. The following weekend, a nurse called to say my mother was getting steadily worse and that she probably would not live through the day. What else could we do except pray and commit the situation to the Lord? Later, the nurse called again to say Mum had passed on a couple of hours before. I believe one day I will join her around the throne of God, and we will praise and worship him together for all eternity.

The second dramatic event was the tragedy that touched the whole nation on September 11, 2001. I spent September 10 at Biola and was at the Los Angeles Airport early on September 11, expecting to get my regularly scheduled plane back to Albuquerque, as I had each week for a couple of years. I intended to put in a full day's work at the office once I arrived back home. My plans changed that day, as did the lives of millions. Since all planes were grounded, I rented a car and began the long drive back to Albuquerque.

During the journey I listened to whatever radio stations I could pick up. Listeners seemed glad talk radio was giving them an outlet for a collective chat at the electronic fireside. Not surprisingly, many listeners were angry; at the same time, they were sharing their disbelief that despite all our sophisticated intelligence-gathering techniques, a tragedy of such cataclysmic proportions could occur in the United States of America.

Over the weeks and months that followed 9/11, we learned of many acts of heroism that occurred on that fateful day and the days following. God's name was mentioned often in previously forbidden public places, and there wasn't a peep heard from the ACLU, Americans United for the Separation of Church and State, or other groups trying to strip all vestiges of Christianity from the public square.

Shortly after the tragic event, I wrote that only eternity will fully reveal what we as a nation learned from that consequential day. Sadly, it appears we haven't learned much. We have returned to our former ways of self-sufficiency and lack of dependence on God. I hope we learn before it is too late that the Savior is the only source of all the blessings we continue to enjoy in this great country of ours.

Struggling with Depression

During my years of doctoral work I struggled with depression. Working on a graduate degree is not an easy thing, and directing a ministry for the homeless on a long-term basis takes an emotional toll. I'm afraid the experience of my depression emerged in some of my writing and even in communications to our donors. At that time, I did not know that one battling depression should tell someone what he is feeling and seek professional help. I did not do that, and in late 2004, I was feeling totally alone, deserted, and abandoned.

I racked my brains for a solution. It seemed as if things were falling to pieces around me, and I was powerless to do anything about it. I felt as if I was coming emotionally unglued and that the weight of the shelter's then entire $1.2-million-dollar annual budget rested on my shoulders. There was the weekly payroll to meet, and late in the week we had nowhere near the funds needed. I visualized the line of people trooping into the office in a couple of days, expecting their paychecks. After all, they had a right to do so. They worked for their money, and it was my responsibility to make sure funds were there to make what they had earned a reality.

To make things worse, our business manager told me in a tense telephone call there were insurance payments and a laundry list of other bills demanding our immediate attention. As if that wasn't enough, I found out that a sizable bequest on which we had been counting to help us navigate through the stormy financial waters leading to the upcoming season of giving would not arrive until the end of the year.

As I worried about the financial needs of Joy Junction, I experienced chest pains and dark spirits. I felt emotionally traumatized and unable to think. I would have liked nothing better than to jump in my car and drive and drive and drive—and forget about Joy Junction. I wondered if it would always be like this. Many years ago, a friend in Santa Fe gave me some wise advice that I mostly dismissed at that time. He said running a nonprofit organization always means dealing with money woes. "You'll never have enough money," he told me.

The question now was how many more times I could deal with the ever-increasing financial strain. Because we were a faith-based ministry and not a social service agency, we did not receive money from any branch of the government (and that was the way I wanted to keep it). But it meant that when we ran short of funds, we could not go to the city council or another government agency, hat in hand, and ask for a financial bailout.

Some people wondered why we couldn't just cut back and live within our means. We did cut back, and we planned a more conservative budget than we might otherwise have done. But we did not even meet that, so we took emergency steps to deal with decreased revenue. We did not want to be examples of the old adage, "When your outgo exceeds your income, it will be your downfall."

But as I thought about where we could prune costs and provide fewer services, I also reflected on the prior months, which had been the busiest ever in my then eighteen years of running Joy Junction. On many nights during the height of summer, we had sheltered two hundred people, and sometimes many more. This was a sharp increase from other years, when even in the depth of winter, with temperatures plummeting to forty degrees and at times even lower, we had only sheltered about 150 people. Unfortunately, the increase did not result in a corresponding increase in income to the shelter. We saw one of the worst summer slumps ever in donations.

While nonprofits locally and nationwide anticipate declines in donations during the summer months, until the events of 9/11 we had things pretty well figured out financially. During the last couple of months of the year we always received more income than we needed to run the shelter. For those months, we put the excess funds into a savings account we could draw from to help get through those traditionally difficult and cash-shy summer months.

In addition, prior to 9/11, we had developed a small group of faithful donors who would give us gifts of stock in the summer to sell as needed. We would apply the funds to meet budget deficits. But the events of 9/11 changed the whole giving cycle, resulting in our generating much less revenue than anticipated to carry into the coming year. On top of this, the crash of the dot-coms very effectively disposed of the formerly disposable funds given to us by generous donors.

The Iraq war served to further compound an already very difficult financial situation. Understandably, people were focused on the Middle East and international events. I understood and supported that different focus while significant international issues were being played out, but local needs continued. Homeless women and families were still in desperate need of a safe place to stay, and while we were glad to be able to provide for those needs, we couldn't do so without community participation.

I issued a plea from the bottom of my heart, not only for Joy Junction, but for all the other rescue missions and faith-based ministries around the nation. More than ever, I said, we needed financial and prayer support from our friends to keep going. We knew that God supplies—there was no question about that—but he also uses his children to do so. The depression I felt did not go away, and I wrote this rather revealing letter to supporters:

> I don't feel a whole lot better about life than I did a couple of weeks ago. While I appreciate some heartfelt messages of prayerful support, lack of money continues to be a major problem at Joy Junction, New Mexico's largest emergency homeless shelter.
>
> As requests for emergency food and shelter have continued in torrents, the funds allowing us to provide those services have just trickled in. That's resulted in our laying off a number of staff and decreasing the number of hours the shelter van is available to provide emergency pick-up service for women and families on the streets. As you can imagine, these decisions weigh on me increasingly heavily—this year for some reason more so than ever. Maybe it's my upcoming 47th birthday and an impending mid-life crisis, or perhaps the stress is something I should expect as a normal part of running a growing ministry.
>
> While some jobs require people to be temporarily on call 24/7, I feel that I'm permanently emotionally and physically tethered to Joy Junction. Whatever I'm doing or wherever I

am, the welfare of the shelter and its guests is always on my mind. Whether it's waking up in the middle of the night wondering how to meet this week's bills, a concern about the welfare of a troubled staff member, or thinking of new and creative ways to share the gospel with our diverse population of homeless guests—Joy Junction is always there.

Now while I know being in that state of mind is not necessarily good, for me it is nonetheless a fact of life. So perhaps you're thinking, "Couldn't he leave Joy Junction? After all, no one is forcing him to stay there!" That's absolutely correct. I founded Joy Junction and remain as its executive director purely because I feel that I am where the Lord wants me to be. With that in mind, I ask for your fervent prayers both for me and this ministry as we continue in our nineteenth year of operation.

It is your prayers that will help determine our survival—or not. Because we are a faith-based ministry and not a social service agency we don't intend to ask the government for funds to bail us out. That leaves us with a couple of options. Either additional money has to come in or we have to make more cutbacks in service and while we'll do that if we have to, the prospect of doing so is very painful.

This was a true expression of my feelings at the time, and I could only pray the Lord would use my words to touch the hearts of our supporters.

Separation and Divorce

In retrospect, it was more than the financial difficulties plaguing Joy Junction causing me to feel depressed. For many years, my wife, Sylvia, and I had been having difficulties in our marriage. There were routine arguments and strained communication resulting, at least in part, from the lack of a shared vision.

The unhappy situation at home made me want to retreat into the peace and security of Joy Junction and my educational pursuits. Yet the more I retreated, the worse things became. Of course, between

Joy Junction and flying back and forth to school, my schedule was very demanding. As my studies progressed, there was more and more reading to do for my Ph.D. For the three months before I took what are called, most appropriately, comprehensive examinations in June of 2002, it seemed that all I did was read and try to master the literature in my field. I read in bed, in the office, on the plane, and in the gym. Wherever I was, I read.

All the reading was partly a way of dealing with the painful reality that Sylvia and I were growing apart. While we had long discussions about what, if anything, was left of our relationship, they did not resolve anything and ended with arguments and the feeling we were only hurting each other. For the sake of the shelter, a possible divorce was something I always resisted.

Finally, in November of 2004, we agreed it would be best if I moved out of the ministry-provided house that had been our family home since the late 1980s. I moved into a very modest residence located on our fifty-two acre property—so modest, in fact, that it did not have a working stove or microwave. While my new living arrangements were sparse and lonely, they were at least peaceful. Basically, I buried myself in my office.

Although I was going through all the motions of running the shelter, issuing news releases and the like and trying to make sure the money kept coming in, I lost heart in what I was doing. I had shut down emotionally. I saw our guests as just people, not as hurting hearts and souls desperately needing the love and compassion the Lord wanted to minister to them through me. Who knows how long I could have gone on like that before having an emotional meltdown?

I kept a small number of close friends and colleagues apprised of my situation and asked them to pray for my family and me. I am particularly thankful for the way the administrative team at Joy Junction supported me during those difficult days. I believe it is important for Christians to be there to listen or offer some kind words to those both in the church and outside undergoing separation or divorce. Why do we seem to ignore their pain or even treat them with contempt due to their problems, when they so desperately need our words of comfort and encouragement?

One day in February, a man appeared at my office door. He said, "Mr. Reynalds, I'm sorry, but I need to serve you these," and he apologetically gave me divorce papers. I shouldn't have been surprised. After all, Sylvia and I had been living apart for fifteen months, and any emotional bond we once shared had waned. We would soon add to an already unfortunate statistic of the number of evangelical Christians who have been divorced.

As a community leader and the longtime director of Joy Junction, I was supposed to be stoic and unmovable. During the months of my separation and subsequent divorce, a steady parade of people trickled in and out of my office throughout the day, seeking help with their needs, apparently not recognizing that I had needs, too.

While my own marriage sadly had fallen apart, Joy Junction was and is all about keeping families together as well as just loving people and giving them hope. The Lord's prompting helped reawaken me to the needs of the hundreds of people and scores of families pouring through Joy Junction, and I realized the Lord's calling on my life had not changed. Only now, I was no longer shut down. I was completely aware of the needs of the downhearted people around me, and I was focused on doing everything I could to provide for them. Although I was unable to save my own marriage, I understand the mission God initially gave me—to keep families together and minister to them as a cohesive unit—is still the foundation of this ministry.

Since then, I have found myself going through a continuing metamorphosis (or maybe *epiphany* would be a better word) in my life. I fell in love with the Lord again and with the people he provided to help me. I agonized with Joy Junction guests when they were hurt and rejoiced with them when they had even small victories—like celebrating a month of being drug- or alcohol-free. A staff member once asked me whether it ever gets any easier seeing the continuous stream of needy, precious humanity flow through our doors. My honest response was "No, it doesn't get any easier. In fact, it gets harder. If you find yourself able to look at our guests without being touched and their pain and plight doesn't gnaw at your soul, then it is time to start looking for another job."

The Lord prompted me through a former staff member to begin writing a series of books that tell the stories of broken individuals who had come to Joy Junction and gotten back on their feet. These coincided with a burning passion to encourage people to quit judging the homeless and writing them off, and instead reach out with the love of Jesus and minister to their deepest needs. I never wanted to be guilty of doing what I heard the main character articulate in the movie *The Book of Eli*: "All those years I'd been carrying that book and reading it every day. I forgot to live by what it said: 'Do more for others more than you'd do for yourself!'"

I have also increased our outreach to the local community. While we have had a presence with the Albuquerque Chamber of Commerce and the Hispano Chamber of Commerce for the last six years, we have increased our attendance at their meetings and functions. I am also determined to share the stories of the homeless and Joy Junction wherever there is an open door. I strongly believe that we have a biblical and societal responsibility to reach out to the less fortunate among us, and that means telling their stories whenever we can.

A significant expansion in our ministry occurred in late 2009. Just before Joy Junction's 2009 banquet with country singer Rockie Lynne, we published our inaugural issue of the *Joy Junction Gazette*. We reported our wish for a lunch wagon to "go mobile," to feed those individuals who, for whatever reason, did not want to come inside Joy Junction or any other homeless facility in Albuquerque. A few days later, longtime Joy Junction friend Victor Jury, Summit Electric CEO, e-mailed me and directed me to a link on eBay, where there was a lunch wagon for sale. He asked me if we would like it. I took a look and was thrilled with what I saw. Vic was gracious enough to buy it for us, and he flew me out to West Palm Beach, where the vehicle was located. Along with a fellow Joy Junction staff member, I drove what became the Lifeline of Hope back from Florida.

Through the lunch wagon we have met and served many wonderful people all over the Albuquerque area. The Lifeline of Hope is a continuing part of my evolving life and spiritual journey.

It is a wonderful experience to see downcast faces take on smiles of delight as they sample a good-sized bowl of chili or soup and receive other essential items, such as personal hygiene articles or blankets, that many of us tend to take for granted.

While providing thousands of nourishing meals monthly to those outside the walls of Joy Junction, the ministry back at the shelter is still growing by leaps and bounds. We are feeding at least ten thousand meals per month and providing about nine thousand nights of shelter. Our Christ in Power Program (CIPP) is active and growing. (More on this program later.) We have a number of graduations each year, which are wonderful occasions. At these ceremonies, we present graduates with certificates of completion and recognize their accomplishments. Graduating from the CIPP is no easy feat, and we want to make it an experience to remember. In addition, we have had a number of baptisms and marriages, which are always very exciting.

What breaks my heart and the hearts of our staff members is when our facility is filled to capacity and we have to turn away people who have no other place to go. We know there is a good chance when we say we are full that these precious souls will have to spend the night on the streets. How can anyone possibly get a restful night's sleep on the ever-increasingly dangerous streets of Albuquerque? At the very least, they would have to sleep with one eye open. With that in mind, we are launching some ambitious expansion plans at our South Valley property that would take care of some of the growing number of people seeking help from us in this difficult economy.

What a ride the last twenty-six-plus years have been at Joy Junction! I am sure as I continue trusting the Lord that the next quarter century and beyond will be even more exciting. I have no plans to retire. When the Lord gives someone a burden to care for hurting people of any kind, that burden must be acted upon. I hope sharing my experiences will help transform a calling into a reality for some of my readers.

When Vision Becomes Reality

When Joy Junction started in 1986, I spent long hours on the phone, calling various Albuquerque social service agencies and telling them that we would soon be open. This did a couple of very important things. First, the other agencies heard about the opening of the shelter from me and not from someone else. Hearing something directly from the person concerned is one of the best ways to fight off any fear and resulting gossip. Second, it was a way to spread the word around town about our ministry and give other agencies the opportunity to refer guests, if they so wished.

Perhaps because of all that time spent on the telephone, a few days before our official opening Joy Junction welcomed its first family. The man had just been paroled from prison. Along with him were his wife and two children. I was happy. They were delighted. Joy Junction was up and running! What happened was that I had received a call from the adult probation and parole people. Officials there heard about our upcoming opening and wondered if we might be able to take in a family prior to opening day. I agreed, on the condition that the family indicated a willingness to help out with building cleanup. The parole officer said the only way this gentleman could get out of prison was if he had a place to stay in a shelter like ours. So the family came, and soon after, another family called. We had guests and were not even open! What a wonderful way to begin our work.

As time passed I was kept busy answering phones, making sure the evening meal was cooked, and teaching the evening Bible study. Every evening it got very late before I knew it, and I had not yet thought about going home.

An article by then staff writer David Morrissey appeared in a September 1986 edition of the *Albuquerque Journal* a couple of days after we opened. It was the start of what was to be a very fruitful relationship with all the Albuquerque media. Here is some of it:

> The Friday dedication of the Joy Junction emergency shelter underscores one of Albuquerque's contradictions—in the midst of a citywide housing boom, a growing number of people have no place to live.
> The Department of Housing and Urban Development says more than 8,000 housing units were built during the last two years in Albuquerque. Another 2,000 units are now under construction.
> There are so many apartments in the city, 15 percent are vacant—a rate twice the national average. At the same time, there are many with no place to call home.
> Workers at Albuquerque missions and emergency shelters say the need is growing.
> A potluck supper at 6 p.m. Friday will show off one effort to meet the needs of the homeless, said the Rev. Jeremy Reynalds, director of the shelter.
> Scheduled to open Oct. 1 [1986], the facility at 4500 2nd St. SW, is located at what was the dormitory of the now-closed Our Lady of Lourdes High School. The building, which is owned by DARE (Drug Alcohol Rehabilitation Enterprises), has been leased to serve as a shelter, said Reynalds.
> Joy Junction will provide both emergency and long-term shelter for single women and families, Reynalds said. The need for shelter for these people in Albuquerque is greatest, he added.
> Prior to the opening of Joy Junction, which will be able to house a maximum of seven families and 10 women, there were only three emergency shelters in the city with facilities to house families. Those shelters, serving Albuquerque's metropolitan area of more than 400,000 people, could handle a maximum of 14 families.
> Joy Junction, a nondenominational ministry, as well as, a shelter, will be funded by donations, Reynalds said. It will

not seek or accept federal, state, or city funds. The shelter especially needs food and bedding, he said.

Reynalds said he expects the shelter to help out those who are "temporarily economically disadvantaged"—people who can be helped to find new jobs and housing.

"Because of the current economic climate there are people using shelters today who never imagined they would need emergency housing," Reynalds said.

Doing Everything at Once

The first month passed quickly, and sometimes I wondered who and what I was. For the first month or so, I was doing everything. I was the shelter's executive director, but I was also working with private donors and the local food bank to make sure there was always something good to feed those the Lord brought our way. I answered the phone and typed all my own letters. In addition, I prepared the evening Bible studies—and occasionally left to go home to my family.

David Morrissey of the *Albuquerque Journal* wrote another piece about Joy Junction on November 27, 1986, a few months after we opened. This time the article profiled one of the first families helped by our shelter. Here is what he wrote:

> Pilgrims at the first Thanksgiving gratefully thanked God for bringing them through a difficult and uncertain year.
>
> Ted and Judy Kotoff will offer much the same prayer as they sit down today for their Thanksgiving dinner in Albuquerque.
>
> The Kotoffs, both 32, are in many ways a typical family. They work hard, try to save their money and want the best for their four-year-old son Jesse.
>
> Thanksgiving is a day they reflect on their blessings. But this year Ted and Judy Kotoff are homeless.
>
> Their Thanksgiving table is at Joy Junction, an Albuquerque shelter for homeless families and single women, where they now live in one small bedroom.
>
> They arrived in Albuquerque three weeks ago from South

Carolina. They lived in a trailer there—sometimes employed, sometimes looking for work. When jobs proved scarce, they headed west.

It was not so much they intended to stop in Albuquerque, Ted Kotoff explained. It was just that here their meager savings ran out.

By chance they heard of Joy Junction, a shelter in the dormitory of the now-closed Our Lady of Lourdes High School at 4500 Second SW, run by the Rev. Jeremy Reynalds.

"We called Jeremy and he took us in," said Ted. "It's been like an oasis in the storm."

"We're both painters," said Judy Kotoff, adding that she was also an electronics technician while Ted had worked as a mechanic and a musician. "We want to work. We're not afraid of hard work." They followed the construction jobs in South Carolina and other states, trying to make enough to settle down, Ted said. But work was infrequent. Stories of high-paying jobs the next state over proved to be wistful thinking.

When construction went bust, the Kotoffs got on with a carnival in South Carolina, operating rides. But when the carnival operator failed to pay them wages they thought they had earned, they decided to make a new start.

In Albuquerque they found temporary jobs as telephone solicitors, earning $4 an hour, 20 hours a week. While staying at Joy Junction, they hope to save enough for an apartment, and find better-paying jobs.

While the homeless are difficult to count and categorize, the federal Department of Housing and Urban Development says they fall into three categories: people with chronic alcohol and drug problems, people with personal crises, such as battered women and runaway children, and people who have suffered severe economic setbacks, such as losing a job.

City officials across the nation report an increase in the number of middle-class Americans forced into emergency shelters through job loss or sudden catastrophic expenses.

Many of these new poor "are just like you and me,"

Reynalds said. "They're not street people, but people temporarily down on their luck."

Ted and Judy Kotoff are thankful today, but they are not satisfied.

If they have their way, the nation's homeless population will be cut by at least one family.

The Homeless Speak

Homeless families are the fastest-growing segment of the homeless population. Sadly, shelters that meet the needs of homeless families are not keeping up with the ever-increasing need for their services.

There is no typical homeless family, because all families are made up of different individuals. During my twenty-six-plus years of running Joy Junction, however, I have seen a number of characteristics common to many homeless families. What follows is a composite picture of a typical homeless family. That means the "Wilson" family does not exist. I have taken many of the most common features I have found in homeless families and woven them into the Wilsons.

A Common Scenario

Let's visit the home of the Wilson family—Robert, Cindy, and their three children. Matthew is seven, Rebecca is five, and JoAnn is two months old. The Wilsons live in Southfield, Michigan, and they have no idea that they will soon be living in Albuquerque, New Mexico. In fact, if you asked them where Albuquerque was, they would probably guess it was in Mexico.

It was a worrisome day for Cindy. Only three months before, the plant cut Robert back to twenty-five hours a week, and there were rumors he might be laid off, along with one hundred others. Twenty-five-hour paychecks had quickly wreaked havoc with the family budget, so much so that, although it was only eleven in the morning on this particular day, three calls from creditors had already come in, each asking when they could expect payment on long-overdue accounts. Cindy began experiencing that panicky feeling; she was getting overwhelmed. She had no idea what they were going to do.

The door opened, and footsteps along the hallway interrupted her thoughts.

"Robert! What are you—"

"Honey, I've been laid off."

"Oh no! What are we going to do?"

"I'll file for unemployment and look for another job. I know we'll make it. We've got to. We've got each other."

The next three months flew by. While the unemployment checks kept the wolf away from the door, that was about all they were doing. There were no frills in the Wilson household, just barely enough to pay the rent and the utilities. Robert and Cindy had always paid their bills promptly and had once enjoyed good credit. But that was no more. The creditors continued calling, and the pressures continued mounting. The once free and easy relationship between Robert and Cindy became tense and bitter. Cindy began blaming Robert for the family's financial problems.

One day, Robert was overcome by deep depression. Slumping into his favorite easy chair, drinking a beer and other stronger beverages, he turned on the television. The phone rang, and Cindy answered.

"Robert or Cindy Wilson, please. This is Bill from the NCI Mortgage Company."

"This is Cindy."

"Cindy, we know you're going through a hard time, but we are a bank and not a welfare agency. Unless you can come up with two of your three outstanding mortgage payments, we'll be forced to foreclose in thirty days. I'm sorry."

Cindy hung up the phone in a daze and rushed back into the living room, where Robert was still sprawled before the television. She spewed out a flood of words she really didn't mean.

"Robert, how can you sit there, slugging down beers this early in the morning, when we're about to become homeless? If you really loved me and the kids, you would be out there looking for work. Why haven't you found a job yet?"

The torrent of words continued. Robert got up slowly, scowled at Cindy, and left the house, slamming the door behind him. He walked angrily down the street, resenting Cindy's words all the way. Why didn't she understand that despite all his attempts to find a job, the work he needed to provide for the family just wasn't there? The economy stank. Sure, he could possibly get a job at a convenience store, but it would pay less than a third of what he had been making at the plant. Why bother? A dark depression began to envelop him. A few minutes later, Robert walked into a local bar and began spending money he didn't have and should not have spent.

Cindy ran to her bedroom, flung herself down on her bed, held the pillow for comfort, and wept bitterly. What had she said?

The hours dragged by with no sign of Robert. At dinner, Rebecca innocently said, "Mommy, where's Daddy? I heard you yelling at him."

"Sweetheart." Cindy's could feel her emotions begin to rise, and she struggled to control herself. "He'll be back soon." With each word, she lost more of her emotions, and her voice rose higher and higher. Rebecca burst into tears and was quickly joined by her brother and sister. Cindy ran to her bedroom, grabbing JoAnn on the way and leaving the other two bewildered and scared children in the kitchen.

At one in the morning Cindy woke to a crying baby. She comforted JoAnn as best she could and ran to check on the other children. They were huddled on the couch with tear-stained faces—fast asleep. Cindy gently placed her children in their beds and returned to an uneasy sleep. She was awakened two hours later by a sheepish Robert, crawling into bed. She reached for him and managed to say between sobs, "Honey, I'm so sorry." They fell asleep in each other's arms, weeping in the midst of a situation over which they had no control.

Robert and Cindy awoke early after a restless night. They prepared breakfast and sent Matthew to school. Rebecca was still sleeping, and JoAnn was gurgling happily. There was time to talk, drink coffee, and get a head start on the day.

Robert spoke first. "Honey, this just isn't working. I've tried. You know I've tried." He started weeping, and Cindy put her arm around him for comfort.

"We could ask my mom and dad," Cindy said.

"No way!" Robert cried. "They were always against us getting married anyway, and they'd love for us to break up. Anyway, they live in public housing and can't have anyone stay with them for more than a few days." Robert suddenly had an idea. "Honey, a few weeks ago, when I was out with the guys, we were just shooting the breeze, and they said there's welding work in Albuquerque, New Mexico. We could—"

"I'm not going to Mexico," Cindy said.

"No, silly," Robert said. "New Mexico, not Mexico. New Mexico's in the United States, stuck between Arizona and Texas. Let's check into it."

The next few days brought a continued barrage of calls from creditors. Robert and Cindy did not even bother answering the phone anymore. What was the point? There was no money to pay the bills. And then a few days later, they did not have to think about the telephone anymore. It was turned off.

One evening, a friend of Robert's came to visit. The conversation quickly shifted to money—or the lack of it.

"Rob, I know there's work in Albuquerque. Welders are getting paid twenty-five dollars an hour. The housing's cheap, and there's plenty of it. Why don't you guys just pack up and go? What've you got to lose?"

A determined look came over Robert's face. "Man, I can't stand this anymore. Cindy, let's do it."

Cindy suddenly recalled something that filled her with more hope than she had experienced in the last few months. "Honey, one of the girls I graduated with from high school moved to Albuquerque. I haven't heard from her in years, but she lives somewhere close to downtown there. I know we could stay with her."

Over the next few days, the Wilsons sold most of their belongings, packed the rest in the dilapidated family station wagon, and set out for Albuquerque. They left Southfield with $350 in their pockets.

About an hour after they started, the radiator began to boil. A few miles later, there was a loud pop, and the car sputtered to a noisy halt.

Robert got out of the car and groaned. There were two flat tires, the radiator was still boiling, and the tailpipe had fallen off. He gave Cindy the bad news.

"I'd better hitch to the nearest gas station," Robert said wearily. "We didn't allow money for car repairs, though."

Five and a half hours and a tow truck later, the Wilsons were on their way again, $250 poorer. Robert said glumly, "There's no way we'll make it to Albuquerque on the money we have left. But let's fill up the tank, get as far as we can, stop at the cheapest motel we can find, and think."

By nightfall, they had covered another two hundred miles, including a brief stop for bologna, mayonnaise, and bread. After checking into a motel, they talked.

Robert said, "Honey, we'll have to stop along the way. I'll work, and we can stay in the missions."

"Missions!" Cindy said, half-frightened and half-angry. "No way! We're not staying in any missions."

"Honey, we might have to, just for a little while, until we can get a few dollars together," said Robert.

They continued their conversation on how the family could best make their way to Albuquerque.

The following morning, after more bologna sandwiches, the Wilson family was on the road again, with thirty-two dollars and a full tank of gas. Nothing was resolved in the motel room discussion, because nothing could be agreed on. The family expedition lasted three weeks, and there were several arguments on the way. Robert and Cindy said many hurtful things to each other in the heat of the moment, and the scars from those hastily spoken words would take many years to heal.

During their trip, minor needs turned into major nightmares. There was no money to buy diapers, and the car's air conditioner broke. Finally, Robert and Cindy saw the signs on the highway they had been waiting for: Welcome to Albuquerque. They hugged and wept for joy. At last! Their long ordeal, they believed, was over.

"Let's go to Twelfth Street, Northwest," Cindy said excitedly, "and we'll find Mary. I know where she lives. Look, I've got the last letter she wrote me, and it says the address right here: 1415 Twelfth Street, Northwest."

The family made their way to the address with much anticipation, but there was no house or apartment, just a parking lot. After asking around, they found no one who even knew who Mary was. After tears of bitter disappointment and a few inquiries into the Albuquerque job market, Robert was convinced there were no welding jobs currently available. The entire family piled back into the car and cried. The Wilsons just sat there, too tired and drained to do anything other than cry—and wait.

Seven hours later, a police officer asked them if he could help. Hearing their story, he said, "There's only one shelter that will take you at this time of night and let you all stay together, and that's Joy Junction." An hour later, Robert, Cindy, and the children arrived at Joy Junction.

A Family Shelter

Because of the shelter's structure, Joy Junction is able to help many families like the Wilsons by providing shelter and keeping the entire family together during a crisis. Unfortunately, shelters like Joy Junction are still very few and far between. Can you imagine how families like the Wilsons would feel if they had to be split up? What would it do to them? It would separate them when they needed each other's support the most.

I hope you are beginning to understand how important family shelters are and how we, as Christians, are biblically obligated to provide more shelters like this one. I reiterate that what you have just read is a composite. While the Wilsons are a fictional homeless family, I drew from characteristics I have noticed in homeless families over a number of years.

The following are actual case histories of some people who stayed at Joy Junction. Some time ago, I distributed a random, unscientific questionnaire to the residents, asking for each respondent's name (optional), family size, highest educational grade reached (or whether the respondent received any college training), home state, occupational training, and current employment status.

I then requested details about how they became homeless, including why friends and relatives were unable to help them, how they felt about being homeless, how they ended up in Albuquerque, whether they planned on staying, and what they would feel like if their families had to be separated in order to stay in a shelter.

Here are some of their responses. I have changed only their names to protect their privacy.

Jane

Jane obtained her GED in prison and has also completed two years of trade school. Her home state is New Mexico. She is qualified to do commercial driving, computer data entry, computer analysis, and other skilled jobs. Jane has been doing all sorts of temporary work, but mostly she has been cleaning and doing general unskilled labor. How did she become homeless?

"At a certain point in my life, I had some trouble with the law over worthless checks. It was an election year, so I was convicted quickly and subjected to the full penalty of the law: forty-two months in the New Mexico Corrections Department. During this period of time, I finished high school and entered college. I had high hopes for reintegration into society. Upon leaving prison, I found it difficult (impossible) to find work, because I had to disclose my parole status. I checked out schools and found that I could not use any credits from prison as a base to continue my education. I had to begin over again at an accredited school.

"I finished my training and also my parole. I was still unable to pass background checks by prospective employers because of my conviction. I did menial jobs when I could find them. I was promptly fired in most cases if any hint of my criminal record came to light.

"Pretty soon, I could not pay rent anymore, so I lived in my car until it was vandalized to the extent that it no longer provided shelter."

Jane continued to tell why her relatives were no longer able to help her.

"When a person has been convicted of a crime, by the time they leave the Department of Corrections, very often they no longer have supportive families, and their 'friends' are often not friends but rather other ex-cons worse off than themselves."

Jane described what she feels like being homeless.

"It feels somewhat humiliating, because there are a lot of general misconceptions about homeless people, for example that none of them want to work, that they are lazy, that they are thieves, and so on. There is a stigma attached to the term 'homeless,' and people do not realize that any kind of disaster could render them in the same position, regardless of careful planning. It is degrading to make people discover this about you, because it alters their opinion [of you] the moment they become aware of the fact."

Many people think that most or all homeless people are transients who aimlessly float across the country. That is not true of most of them, including Jane, who was born in Mountainair, New Mexico. She talked about a common shelter practice: separating families.

"I am currently not living with my husband, because he is in the Corrections Department, but if we were together, we would prefer living in our car to being separated. To me, homelessness is a temporary living condition that is hard to overcome because of financial setbacks and job search problems. I would not stay in a women's shelter while my husband was forced to stay in the streets, [his] car, or another shelter. I would stay with him until it is possible to rent for ourselves again, regardless of the circumstances."

Jane had an interesting perspective on the need for more family shelters to be built around the United States.

"I think there should be more shelters built, but I also feel, because of the immense concern over homelessness, that it is important to make the public, and especially the church congregations, aware that their interaction and help (not financial, necessarily) in counseling, fellowship, and job opportunities is vital to the successful rise of a family from the despair, isolation, hopelessness, and depression of homelessness."

Steve and Maria

Steve and Maria had one child on the way; Maria was seven months pregnant. Steve had an associate degree in English, and said, "My wife has a sixth-grade reading level but supposedly graduated high school." Steve's home state was California, and Maria's was New Mexico. Steve said he was trained in sales, cooking, cashiering, a little computer programming, data processing, and typing. Lately, he had been doing a little cooking and cashiering.

In his own words, Steve told how he became homeless.

"We tried to make it in California, but I was unable to find a job. The money Maria got from welfare for her pregnancy wasn't enough to live on, so we lost our place."

Steve said that while relatives did what they could, it still was not enough. "Most of my friends were unable to help, because their homes were full or their parents wouldn't allow them to." He painted a graphic picture of the horrors of homelessness. "It's really terrible. I do not know how I am going to take care of my wife and my soon-to-be-born child. I do not know from one day to the next if we are going to have a place to stay or food to eat. I feel absolutely helpless and worthless, because I can't provide for my family."

Steve said if things work out in Albuquerque, "We'll be staying for a while." Asked how he would feel if his family had to be separated to stay in a shelter, Steve responded, "I wouldn't like that at all. My wife has a history of medical problems, and I would be afraid that something would happen. I would sooner sleep on the streets, where I could keep an eye on her, than stay in a shelter, separated, where I couldn't."

Steve stressed the importance of more family shelters being built around the United States. "The number of homeless families is growing, but there is nowhere for them to go. In my hometown in California, there are no shelters for families, and only a few for men and women, other than the battered women's shelter."

Tracy

As I collected case histories and did my questionnaire, every person I asked said they would not stay in a shelter if they had to be separated from their family. Minnesota-born Tracy was no exception. She said it would be too lonely to be separated from her family, and she just would not do it. If she had to be separated, "I'd sleep when I could and travel when I had to, but no shelter."

Tracy had two years of college and was trained in technical-electric assembly. She was receiving Social Security disability and said she became homeless through a drop in her income. Illness caused her to quit working and start receiving Social Security.

"Through Social Security," Tracy said, "my income dropped to half of what I was bringing in per month. To compensate for the lack of money, I had to move to an apartment that was a lot smaller and cheaper than what I was living in." She still was not making it, so she came to Albuquerque after friends told her there was cheaper housing and an overall lower cost of living than in Minnesota. "So I saved my money and drove here in two days.

"Homelessness is very depressing. I miss my home and my things around me. Just to brush my teeth seems a chore, because I have to dig through everything to get my toothbrush. That is, if there is room at the sink even to get it done. I get angry very easily over little things because I cannot even have a minute to myself. Everyone needs a little space to call their own."

Tracy said that while she had relatives, they could not help her because they were on limited incomes. "They're retired, but maintain their homes, as they're paid for. They can't afford to have one more person to feed." She said it would be a blessing for everyone if there were more family shelters around the United States.

David and Karen

David and Karen moved from Big Springs, Texas, to Albuquerque, for entirely different reasons: their eldest daughter's health. David was a high-school graduate, but Karen left school in the tenth grade. They had two daughters. David's home state was Texas, and Karen was a native New Mexican. David said he was willing to do "anything possible" in the construction field.

About his daughter, David said, "We can get more help for her here. She's handicapped with epilepsy, and Texas was overmedicating her." David and Karen said relatives could not help them out in their plight, and they did not have any friends in Albuquerque.

"Homelessness is depressing," David said. "No privacy. But thankfully we have a roof over our heads, meals for my kids, and a place to sleep." Asked if he would separate from his family in order to have a place to stay, David said he would not. "My girls need both of us, and we need them." David and Karen agreed there was a need for more centers like Joy Junction around the country "because there are a lot of families that need the help and shelter."

Sam and Deborah

Sam and Deborah did not have any children, and they both graduated from high school. Sam was a truck driver, and Deborah worked in factories and kitchens, but both had been unemployed for a year. They said they became homeless through divorce.

Sam said that neither friends nor relatives were able to help them because "Neither one of us gets along with our families very well, and most of our friends couldn't help." The couple said it was hard being homeless, but there had been some very nice people who had helped them along the way.

Deborah said that Sam's former employment resulted in their coming to Albuquerque. "Sam used to drive a truck through Albuquerque, and he liked the town, so we decided to move here. Yes, we are planning to stay." Sam and Deborah said they felt it was important that there be more family shelters built around the United States, as many states don't have shelters where the whole family can stay together.

David and Jean

David and Jean were also residents at Joy Junction. David had a ninth-grade education, and Jean was a high school graduate. They were from Texas and had no children. David said he was trained to do landscaping, sprinkler systems repair, construction, paint and bodywork, and plastering.

Jean recounted how they became homeless. "My husband lost his job in El Paso because the company went out of business. We lost our apartment through lack of money." She said they stayed with friends for a couple of days, until they made enough money to buy bus tickets to Albuquerque.

"We got in Tuesday and went to the Albuquerque Rescue Mission, and they told us about Joy Junction. We called, and they came and picked us up. The people here are very nice and also very polite and understanding and caring." Jean explained why they could not get any more help than they did from friends. "I didn't want to stay there, because they were into drugs." Their family in El Paso could not help them, because they were already supporting other children.

The couple came to Albuquerque "to stay and get a good job and start a new life here." Jean said, "It's scary and horrible to be homeless, because living out in the streets you could ... trust no one out there. People are getting mugged in front of the El Paso Rescue Mission and the Salvation Army. We are very thankful for Joy Junction having us here."

Jean believed there were more job opportunities in Albuquerque than in El Paso, and the couple planned on staying here. "It will take time, but with God's help, we are going to get back on our feet again," they said. She said she believed it was very important that more family shelters be built in the United States to give homeless families with children a safe place to stay.

More Homeless Speak

Rachel

Rachel never planned on a life of drinking. Who does? But it happened to her nonetheless. She told me that in her younger years, she would notice a bedraggled homeless woman and flinch. "We callously called her a 'bag lady' back then," Rachel said. "I was appalled at how one could allow oneself to get that way. I pitied her."

Other images bought similar feelings to mind—like when Rachel would see a drunk man stumbling along or lying in a doorway, or a drunk woman carousing in a bar. But she drifted into a life of drinking and drugs very similar to the ones she had not so long ago pitied. She said she could not really pinpoint a definitive experience that led to her decades of drinking. "I'd often find myself drinking and cogitating about all the poor decisions I'd made in the past that were affecting me now, and instead of changing my ways, I became more morose about it as I drank."

Rachel recalled some still vivid instances of those alcohol-ridden years. She would wake up in the hospital emergency room with no idea why or how she got there. She would be dragged into a police station in shackles or just fall down drunk at parties. Many times, she would have no idea how long a particular blackout had lasted. Most distressing was what this lifestyle did to her family. She would break promises to her daughter or tell her to go across the street to play in the park while she drank in the bar. She even walked away from two long-term relationships because she knew that continuing them meant getting help for her alcoholism and drug abuse.

Here is a description of what Rachel's life was like in the 1960s in southern California, when she was in her teens and twenties: "You couldn't imagine the availability of recreational drugs that were in plentiful supply during the hippie era. LSD wasn't even illegal yet when I started taking it. Pot, acid, mushrooms, and peyote were there for the asking, with the groovy people I hung with to turn on and drop out. Psychedelics were cool. Acid was my favorite. I didn't feel rebellious really, just liberated mentally and artistically."

Rachel used drugs for many years, even into her fifties, although alcohol "became king of the party," as she put it. How did alcohol affect her? "It's an amazing accelerant for burning bridges, or stomping out after an argument to end up in a bar with the old 'I'll show them' attitude, or making bar acquaintances for the sole purpose of having rounds bought by others. I thought I was asserting control and being independent and doing what I pleased, regardless of the consequences. It was a way of life, such as it was, with the 'they'll get over it when I sober up' attitude."

But this description barely scratched the surface of her alcohol-infused life. She went through alcoholic treatment programs four times, usually at the request of others who wanted her to get help. She said, "I knew in my heart and soul that I needed to do something, though I was averse to admitting there was a problem I couldn't handle myself. Getting sober for others was short lived at best, a year here, six months there. With varying lengths of sobriety under my belt, so to speak, I would invariably go retrograde and find myself drinking, drunk, and dazed in short order again and again."

Rachel always balked at step two of the Alcoholics Anonymous creed, which is to ask for help from a higher power. "Greater power? Sure. Sanity? Elusive. I attempted to find the strength in myself to carry on my sobriety. Ha! Obstinate and independent minded, I struggled for years, though I knew in my heart of hearts that there had to be a God. Seeing the mountains, the ocean, and the sky all around us, who could deny the divine maker of the universe? As perverse and insidious as alcohol's grip was on me, my spirituality was always there within. But I had shoved it to the wayside, the proverbial back burner, for the pursuit of the ultimate party!"

As a result, Rachel said, God's grace allowed her to flounder, because she was too proud to ask for help. Of course, pride comes before a fall, and even though she was lost, she did not realize how far she had fallen. Among other things, she had lost her home, her jobs, her possessions, her self-respect, and the trust of her loved ones.

Her daughter told her, "Mom, when are you going to get help? I'll help you; I'll take you to treatment—anything! Can't you stop? I don't want your grandkids growing up knowing Gramma only as a drunk! You've fallen down, stumbled, and slurred in front of them enough." Despite that desperate plea, Rachel continued drinking for years more. She said, "My daughter's voice, when on yet another of her Mommy rescue missions, resounds in my ear: 'Mom, grow up, the party's over!'" All in all, Rachel's drinking lasted forty years.

Finally, all of Rachel's options were exhausted, and her daughter suggested she call Joy Junction. "Actually, she called for me, as I was sobering up that morning at her house. Thank God, it was her last rescue mission! That was a little over two years ago. Coming to Joy Junction, I thought I'd hang out a week or two. Alcohol had taken so much from me. I was grateful to have a place to lay my bleary head at night. I felt as though all my guardian angels were heaving great sighs of relief."

While at Joy Junction, Rachel was reintroduced to the Bible. Many of the Scriptures she read reminded her of her mother and her home of so many years ago. Rachel is now on staff at Joy Junction as part of our maintenance team. Her daughter told her, "Mom, I'm so glad you're at Joy Junction now. I don't have to worry about you anymore."

Rachel said, "I thank God for all that Joy Junction has helped me do through the love of God and community. I also praise God that I still have the wherewithal to be able to share this with you and that my daughter never gave up on me. Her love helped guide me when I was too blind to see the way myself."

We are so proud of Rachel and all she has allowed the Lord to do in her life. She is an ongoing testimony to the goodness and power of God. Looking at her transformed life demonstrates what the Lord can do when we turn everything over to him.

Mary

Mary is a Joy Junction life recovery program graduate. She recalled vividly the embarrassment and humiliation she suffered in years past when she had to use the bathroom. At one point, pregnant and suffering from a urinary tract infection, Mary went into a restaurant and asked to use the bathroom. She was not allowed to do so. Mary was in such dire straits she ended up relieving herself behind a dumpster in the parking lot.

"It was degrading," Mary said. "The people looked at me as if I was the scum of the earth. All I wanted to do was use the bathroom. It's not like they couldn't see I was pregnant, yet they still treated me like I was scum." She experienced disapproving looks and similar refusals at many other restaurants and businesses.

Mary said, "It felt as if they were treating me less than human. I felt embarrassed."

The trauma Mary experienced is multiplied numerous times by countless numbers of the most needy among us. It is so important that this public attitude be brought to the attention of as many people as possible. What can you do to help?

Ann, Ava, and Amber

Joy Junction operates a faith-based, multistage Christ in Power Program (CIPP) that revolves around the changes necessary for our guests to get back on their feet. Graduating members of Joy Junction's nine-month life recovery program receive their certificates at a very special ceremony. While some smile, others are very nervous. They all work hard to complete their program, and they all deserve their special moment of recognition.

People come to Joy Junction for many reasons. For some residents, it is the difficult economy and the lack of ability to cope with life in our ever-increasingly stressful society. Others struggle with drugs, alcohol, poor money management, poor parenting skills, and mental health issues.

Three of our graduates told us a little bit about their lives and what being in the program meant to them. Pray for all of them and their continued success.

Ann was an abuse and rape victim. Before she came to Joy Junction, she lived with her cousin and tried to find a job. Unable to find employment, she was asked to leave her cousin's apartment and ended up at the shelter. Ann described how she felt on her arrival at Joy Junction. "When I got here, I was nervous and scared, because I didn't know anyone and I was alone."

Although she was alone, she felt safe, and she quickly realized she did not want to leave the security of Joy Junction and deal with the uncertainties and dangers lurking on downtown Albuquerque streets. It didn't take Ann long to realize that joining the CIPP would be the right decision for her.

Although the CIPP was sometimes difficult for her and initially she felt that God wasn't there for her, Ann feels much differently now. Most importantly, she's gotten closer to the Lord and has developed better life skills. She said she knows also that if she needs to talk, she can share her heart with our staff as well as directly with the Lord.

She said, "The program has taught me how to handle things better at a job. I also know that everyone here cares and loves me along with God, and that I also have a roof over my head and food to eat. It has helped me to feel safe here."

Ann said she is so happy she finished something she started without having to have someone push her through it. "Thank you, guys, for being there for me and helping me through my problems and the negative things I have gone through most of my life."

Ava also told us her story. Mother to three beautiful children, she and her husband have been at Joy Junction for a little more than a year. Ava came to Joy Junction because she had never had a real job. Her "employment" had been trafficking drugs. After serving her time, an extended stay with relatives didn't work out for the family, and they were eventually forced to leave.

This was not Ava's first stay with us, for she recalled being here when she was nine years old, after her mother fled an abusive relationship. She lost her dad due to alcohol when she was eight and had lived on her own since she was fourteen years old. She admitted dabbling with drugs and alcohol even back then, but she said addiction was never a "real" problem.

She did say, though, that she had been "confused" about God for all her life. When she lost her mother, she blamed God and asked why he would make her suffer. After joining the CIPP and graduating seven months later, Ava now has a different perspective. She said not only did she learn about the Lord's love for her, but, very importantly for her recovery and self-esteem, she was also able to finish something she started.

She added, "I know God brought me here to strengthen my relationship with my family and get to know him better. I am very grateful for Joy Junction and what they have taught me. It is not just a homeless shelter; it is more like a family."

Sometimes it takes more than one attempt to successfully complete the CIPP. Amber first came to Joy Junction with a meth and alcohol addiction. She had also endured and finally left an almost two-decade-long abusive relationship.

Her first time around, Amber completed about half the CIPP before she left. It wasn't easy for her expanding family. She got pregnant after leaving Joy Junction and, along with her daughter and boyfriend, moved from motel to motel for a while. Eventually, her boyfriend obtained employment, and the family was able to get an apartment, just before the birth of her son.

More problems lay ahead. During her pregnancy and the subsequent birth of her son, Amber was having serious kidney issues, while her boyfriend was having problems with his gallbladder. She had five surgeries on her kidneys, and her boyfriend was also hospitalized. As a result, they ended up behind in their rent and lost their apartment. After this, they came back to Joy Junction and rejoined the program.

Amber said, "I hadn't finished high school, and I've gone to college a couple of times but never finished anything that I have started. Finally, I finished something—the CIPP. Being on the CIPP and successfully finishing it has brought up my self-esteem, and [it] makes me feel good to help people."

Amber has also been clean from her meth addiction for a couple of years, and that, she said, makes her "feel good." As a CIPP graduate, she is continuing for the moment to serve those individuals in similar circumstances to those she was in not so long ago.

She said, "To give back to the community of the homeless is a great honor, and it makes me appreciate everything Joy Junction has taught me and done for me."

With the Lord's help and the support of his people, Ann, Ava, and Amber will continue to succeed. To those who prayerfully and financially support Joy Junction, thank you. Without you, these stories wouldn't be possible.

Brenda and Zach

Brenda was married to a man who abused her. I am glad she left her abuser, because if she had stayed, she might not be alive today. I learned that the misery that characterized her first marriage started with emotional and mental abuse.

"He told me I was useless," Brenda said. "I was always being corrected and reprimanded; nothing was ever good enough. Then it turned physical. Being slapped and hit by a man three times my size was more than I could take. The police were no help. When I got the courage to leave, he became completely obsessed and possessive."

After Brenda married Zach, her abusive ex-husband tracked her down. "He made our lives a living hell," she said. The couple decided to relocate from the South and move to the West Coast to live in a state where there were more job opportunities. But unexpected events led them to Joy Junction in Albuquerque. Even though this wasn't where they expected to be, Brenda says, "It's a true comfort and a blessing for both of us to be here at Joy Junction, knowing that we are safe and our identity is protected."

Zach took up the story. He said the couple left their former state with "all our cherished possessions." They sold their furniture and electronics to finance the impending journey. The trip was pretty uneventful until they arrived at a truck stop just west of Amarillo, Texas.

Zach said, "We had spent the night in our van and had been in and out of the truck stop's store a number of times. We ran in once more, just before we were going to leave, and we came out to find our van gone—along with Brenda's purse, which contained all our money, IDs, and debit cards, not to mention all our possessions—pictures, kids' yearbooks, and precious keepsakes from both our families."

Brenda added, "Like a dummy, I had put the keys on the floorboard. Someone must have been watching, because we were only inside for a couple of minutes."

Fortunately, much-needed help was on the way. A Christian family heard about the couple's predicament and offered them a place to stay in their barn, as well as food, in exchange for helping out at their alpaca ranch. The same family, Zach said, also rescued animals from all over the Southwest. Zach said they felt so blessed by the kindness of strangers, "yet not surprised at how the Holy Spirit moves."

The family also provided Zach and Brenda clothing, luggage, and personal hygiene items. They stayed with this family for just over two weeks. While they went on a business trip, they were able to drop Zach and Brenda at Joy Junction.

Zach and Brenda said, "The love and acceptance we have found here has been a true blessing from God. As we pray and lift up our need for bus tickets [out West], we know in our hearts that God will provide. [He will help us] both with our immediate needs of shelter and food, and also for our transportation needs."

In the meantime, Zach and Brenda have joined Joy Junction's Christ in Power Program. Like many others, life has dealt them some hard blows, but they are not buckling underneath them. They feel that what the CIPP has to offer will help strengthen their relationship with the Lord and give them a new beginning—a beginning that will benefit them for many years to come. As Zach said, "If it had not been for the love and assistance of Joy Junction, we do not know what, or where, we'd be."

Without friends who prayerfully and financially support the ongoing ministry of Joy Junction, there would have been no refuge for Zach and Brenda to come to and feel the peace and love of the Lord Jesus Christ. Nor would there have been a place to stay and nourishing meals to eat. I continue to be amazed by God's grace and the miraculous transformations and life healings we see at Joy Junction on a daily basis.

Carl

Carl didn't stay at Joy Junction the night I met him. Judging from his condition, I have a suspicion he probably stayed outside or in an abandoned building somewhere. But I believe he went to bed on a full stomach.

When my friend David and I met Carl, it was on the corner of First and Central, in downtown Albuquerque. We went downtown to get a cup of coffee and a bite to eat after the Saturday evening service at Joy Junction. We had a great time of fellowship and some good food and were within a few feet of my car when Carl, wobbling along on a cane, entered our lives.

He seemed to recognize me immediately. Slurring his words he said, "You're Jeremy from Joy Junction, right?" I acknowledged I was, and Carl, who was visibly drunk and with the stench of alcohol assaulting me as he spoke, said something to the effect of "You want to give me some money so I can buy food?"

I let Carl know that we didn't give money but would be happy to buy him a meal if he wanted. All I could see across the street was a sushi restaurant (which Carl declined), but then my friend remembered we had just passed a restaurant that sold pizza. David asked him if he wanted pizza, and Carl said no. He did, however, want something to drink. We walked across the busy street, watching him carefully to make sure he didn't get run down, and entered the sushi restaurant, where David bought Carl a bottle of cold water.

After David handed our new friend the water, Carl looked around as if considering his options. This time he said he was hungry and would like something to eat. The idea of pizza seemed more appealing to him now. We walked the few hundred feet to the pizza restaurant. Carl did not want to sit down inside, and since we were worried he might wander off, David stayed outside and talked with him while I went inside to order a couple of slices of pepperoni and cheese pizza.

I came outside the restaurant and saw that Carl was looking carefully at David's college ring, which he had taken off at Carl's request for him to see up close. I tried to engage Carl in some limited conversation, but even that was too much for him to cope with that night, struggling as he was in his addled alcoholic stupor.

I wasn't really sure what we were supposed to do next, but I knew the Lord had this precious man encounter David and me (out of everyone else he could have run into) for a reason. With that in mind, it seemed it would be a good idea to pray. David placed his hand gently on Carl's shoulder. Even that soft but apparently unexpected touch startled Carl enough to make him jump as if he had been shocked by a high-voltage electric current. He got up from his chair with difficulty as if he was about to leave.

David persuaded him to sit down again, and we prayed a simple prayer of faith for Carl, asking the Lord's to bless and protect for him. After that, we looked directly at him and said we had to go, but we told him to stay right where he was until his pizza arrived. He didn't promise, but neither did he move. I was prayerfully optimistic!

I don't know what more we could have done for Carl. The rescue missions downtown were full, and there was no more room at the inn at Joy Junction, either. The county jail has not offered protective custody for many years. Carl was out of options.

It would have been easy to dismiss Carl as just a drunk, a bum, or a vagrant. The Carls of this world make many people nervous. They are also an embarrassment to some in city government, because they are a visible reminder of a side of our city some want to keep hidden.

Many of us would say, "He needs to get a job and get his act together." Such an attitude enables us to erect a wall of self-righteousness and justify our unwillingness to help. But before judging Carl and writing him (and hundreds of thousands like him) off, we should ask what experience he suffered that may have played a major role in him looking to alcohol for solace and comfort. Was he abused, emotionally devastated, raped, abandoned, or made to suffer any one of a myriad of similar horrors?

Or was Carl someone suffering from mental illness? Perhaps he was lost to the system and could not afford the medication that could calm his troubled mind. Because of a lack of resources, many are reduced to spending their days shuffling along city streets and enduring embarrassed, nervous looks, a few snickers, and the continuous barking of orders to "move on."

I hope and pray the Lord brought peace to calm Carl's troubled soul. Whatever we think of the Carls we encounter, they are very precious in God's eyes, and they are people for whom the Lord Jesus Christ shed his blood and died upon the cross of Calvary.

Janice and Lonnie

This is not a story with a happy ending, at least not yet. This tale is still unfolding. But it needs telling, because it is happening in our city and in cities all over America.

Sitting on the curb by a shopping cart overflowing with belongings, they were hard to miss. I met the engaging but physically and emotionally worn Janice and Lonnie on Sunday while at Bullhead Park, located behind the Veterans Hospital in Albuquerque. We were there as part of Joy Junction's new Lifeline of Hope meal outreach.

After we gave them sack lunches (for which they were ravenously hungry), sodas, and blankets, I asked them if they would tell me some of their story. They graciously agreed to a brief interview. I learned that Janice and Lonnie are close friends and provide much-needed support and encouragement to each other. They said they have lived for years on and off at Bullhead Park. I asked Janice to tell me how she feels living there.

"It's not fun," she said, coughing. Janice said that while she has been asked to leave by the police on a few occasions, they are, on the whole, pretty kind to her. They even ask her if she and Lonnie are doing okay—that is, as okay as you can be living in a park.

Lonnie told me he has lived at Bullhead Park for five years. Before that, he worked at a local apartment complex as a groundskeeper. I asked him what happened, and he admitted he likes to drink. He quit his job and went to California and then Texas before winding up back in Albuquerque. He said he doesn't go to a homeless shelter because it's "too far."

Janice ended up living at Bullhead Park because when she had an apartment and got a disability check, "I had a lot of friends over … and I got thrown out, and now I'm having a hard time getting another place to live."

When the weather gets down to bone-chilling freezing, Janice said, "We just … brrr." Lonnie said, "We've got plenty of blankets, but it still gets cold." As he spoke, the thought of my comfortable, thermostat-controlled house on the other side of town flashed in my mind. How grateful I was for the security it offers me on very cold nights.

Janice added, "You just wrap up and do the best you can."

Lonnie said, "Body heat, you know."

I asked Janice and Lonnie what hope they saw for the months and years ahead. Janice said, "I'm hoping I can do a little bit better. I get a monthly check, but it's not enough, and I got kicked out of my apartment, because I was letting all of my homeless friends come over and stay with me. I got kicked out not for nonpayment, because I paid my rent, because I do get a monthly check."

I told Janice it almost sounded as if she was trying to run her own homeless agency. Laughing, she turned to Lonnie and said, "I had a lot of people living there, didn't I? About five people one night."

I asked Janice what she would say to individuals who routinely tell me that people like her want to be homeless. She said, "I think they need to come out here and be homeless for a while. Like I said, I get a little monthly check, but it's not enough to really go around. The people who say we want to be homeless are crazy. Because it's cold outside."

Lonnie picks up cans to make a living. He said, "I do all right with cans, and people give me money, food, you know … They help me out. I got my life pretty good, you know." I asked Lonnie whether he would prefer continuing to live in Bullhead Park or if he would really like to live in a house. He said he plans to live in an apartment once he gets his ID and Social Security card, which had been lost along with his wallet, but he can't do that right now.

To those who write off Janice and Lonnie as just a couple of bums who choose to live in the park, Janice says, "Just because we're homeless, we're not bums." Lonnie would tell them, "Why not spend a whole week here, just one week, and then you can call me a bum." Janice added, "Try it for one day. Go out picking up cans all day." She said it was not fun.

Janice said, "I'm working on it. I'm gonna get back on my feet. It might take me another month. Thank you all for the sandwich. We were hungry. We were just thinking about what we were going to eat. Thank God, we were so hungry."

Lonnie added, "Yeah, and here you guys come on over."

Janice and Lonnie's plight touched me deeply. At one point some years ago, I would have quickly dismissed their circumstances as being the result of a series of poor choices. I can no longer do that, but how easy it is to feel justified with such a quick dismissal.

Many would judge Lonnie and Janice while neglecting to find out their story and starting to form a relationship with them. Befriending them without judgment and getting beyond their external circumstances and appearance could play a major part in helping them permanently get back on their feet. After all, isn't that what Jesus would do?

Roger

Stepping outside into the cold, predawn hours of Thanksgiving Day, I prepared to head over to Joy Junction. I was thinking about Roger, an Albuquerque resident whose home has been a local park for a couple of years. He told me living in a park is sometimes scary.

"You don't know who's going to come up behind you," he told

me. "You don't know who's going to come up on top of you, you don't know if the cops are going to come get you, you don't know if someone's going to stab you or beat you, and you don't know what's going to happen. So, a lot of times you have to sedate yourself. You drink to deal with anything that's going to happen."

Roger said it would be tough getting back on his feet again. "You get labeled, and then sometimes you get associated with other people. The police officers see you as a bad guy, but you're not the bad guy. You try to take care of yourself, and you try to do what you can to move on. But sometimes it's not that easy."

Without wanting to pry, I asked Roger if he would feel comfortable telling me what caused his home to be a park. He alluded to "something tragic," and added, "You never thought it would happen to you, and it did happen to you. I guess maybe I'm trying to escape the situation, trying to think, 'This couldn't have happened, 'cause this is not me.'"

It was obvious Roger's new life was a dramatic departure from the way he used to live. He said, "It's difficult when you experience a life of having everything you want and then going to have nothing of what you want. It's tough." Roger said that you end up building your own "family" when you live on the streets. And with those people, he said, "You're always going to be safe."

Roger said, "There's a lot of good people who, for whatever reason, end up out here. I think they can be fixed, but a lot of times it has to do with friendship." He said being regarded as a "bum" by some of the people he encounters hurts. "You get a little resentful and sometimes, depending on your lifestyle and what you've been through ... I don't know, maybe it's easier not to even try and get back on your feet."

Roger is appreciative of ministries like Joy Junction and others that provide a place to stay, hot, nutritious meals, and an array of other services. But the recovery process is still hard. "You're trying to replace yourself with something different than your present situation, and it's more of a mental thing, so it's real tough sometimes." I offered Roger a place at Joy Junction, but he is not ready to take that step.

One thing is for sure: Roger's healing will be found in a relationship with the Lord Jesus Christ. Maybe the Lord will reach out supernaturally to Roger to heal that broken heart, and maybe God will choose to use one of his children to do so. If God chooses to use us, will we accept the assignment or pass by on the other side of the road?

A Joy Junction staff member said, "Either way you look at it, homelessness is not something to fear, scorn, or disdain. It is an opportunity for healing, a chance to help and be more like Jesus by treating our fellow men appropriately. 'Do to others as you would have them do to you.'"

Greg

He didn't know it at the time, but Greg was about to find out the truth of the Scripture, "Your enemy the devil prowls around like a roaring lion looking for someone to devour" (1 Peter 5:8). Sometimes the enemy uses those you may least expect, like your coworkers.

Greg and his family moved to Albuquerque from Reno, Nevada, for a new job in Rio Rancho. Wanting to fit in with his coworkers, Greg started using crack cocaine and became addicted. After a lot of anguish and turmoil caused by Greg's drug abuse, he quit his job. Soon, there was no more money. As a result, along with his wife Mary and their three children, Greg came to Joy Junction.

Hoping to permanently conquer what had become a life-controlling and family-threatening addiction, Greg joined Joy Junction's life recovery program, the Christ in Power Program. "My wife told me for a long time to get help, and I figured this was the place to get it. While on the CIPP, I learned more about God and myself than I ever could have on my own."

While Greg had been doing well, he was about to hit a serious bump in the road. "As I was getting better with my addiction and closer to God, I hit a 'self-destruction relapse' button." Greg relapsed twice, both times leaving Joy Junction property before succumbing to his old addiction. He said, "That caused me to almost lose my family twice."

When he used drugs, he had no idea what he was doing to his family. "My wife and I have three children. I would spend our money and then tell my kids no about going to the store. I would always put them last, but they never put me last. For almost two years, I did this to my family. My wife would even try to hide money."

By God's grace, Greg worked through his issues. After we saw the progress he was making, we offered him a staff position at Joy Junction. Greg accepted, and he worked for us and lived on-site for quite a while. When another, higher paying job offer came along, he felt it was time to move on.

Reflecting on that time in his life, Greg said, "During my stay at Joy Junction, I received a lot of compassion and a desire to develop a closer relationship to God. The staff here taught me a better way to live with God in my life. After I learned to love my family again, I got a better job. I worked for my family, not for me. I put my notice in and went to work at a tire shop."

Excited about their future, Greg, Mary, and the kids never dreamed what trials lay ahead. Greg suffered a massive heart attack. He recalled asking the Lord for his help. After one year of recuperation, he was able to return to work, but he ended up with a hernia and a nine-month recovery period. As a result, the family got behind on their rent and was evicted. That caused their return to Joy Junction.

Surprisingly, Greg isn't angry about all the ups and downs he's experienced in life. He said his current stay at Joy Junction has been the most rewarding ever for him and his family. "We have more love for God, which reflects on to the other people staying here who want that same experience for themselves. I praise Joy Junction for the reason they're here—not for the symbol of homelessness, but the symbol of love and of the hope of Jesus Christ for all who come here!"

It is such a joy to see Greg's and Mary's happy, smiling faces at our church services. It is thrilling to report that Greg has now been drug-free for years, and he has never relapsed. I am also grateful that when Greg and Mary had no place to stay, they knew to call Joy Junction. When they are ready and able, we want to see them return to self-sufficiency. Meanwhile, we believe that every day they live and serve the Lord while they stay at Joy Junction is a step in that direction.

Jennifer

Since she was a child, Jennifer prayed for a baby boy. The Lord fulfilled the desire of Jennifer's heart. But about a month later, the baby's father left. Jennifer said he couldn't handle the attention being lavished on his new son, Joshua. He did, however, come by weekly to spend about a half hour with his son.

Those visits decreased and then stopped entirely. When Joshua was three or four years old, his dad would tell him he would come and pick him up for the weekend. Jennifer said, "Joshua would get his overnight bag and sit on the curb and wait for his father, who would never show up. After a while, he would come in with tears and ask me why, and it would crush my heart." As that same scenario played out over and over, Jennifer said resentment and anger followed.

Jennifer recalled that when Joshua was four, she met a man who was a chef. They started dating, and both Jennifer and Joshua fell in love with him. Her son's affection, and the fact that the three of them went camping and fishing together, thrilled Jennifer. She was delighted that the man she had chosen to be in her life loved her son as his own.

But there was a side to this man that Jennifer didn't know, and it didn't surface until they had both gotten a job at a local bar. At first her life with this man was fun and exciting, but it quickly became a nightmare. The man she thought loved her was drunk 24/7. Black eyes and a smashed head became the norm for Jennifer.

One night, it was especially bad. "As we were walking, he turned around and pushed me in the chest, and I flew backward. I cracked my head wide open. I heard my son's blood-curdling scream and managed to run to him. I just couldn't imagine what he felt like, seeing my face and clothes drenched in blood. I just held him as he cried."

Jennifer left this man, but more trauma was on the horizon. Initially comforting, the trauma took the form of a male friend Jennifer had been supporting—until she caught him lying, cheating, and stealing. Although Jennifer told him to leave, he began stalking her, making unwanted calls, and even going to her place of employment. Desperate, Jennifer moved. That wasn't enough, though, as he still found her.

At that point, he started abusing Joshua emotionally and Jennifer physically.

Jennifer recalled a terrifying incident when he broke into her apartment in the middle of the night. He wanted to use the phone. As she had to get up at four, Jennifer told him to hurry up. "He threw the phone at me, and it hit me in the temple. All I felt was warm fluid rushing down my face, and I heard my son running into the room. Fed up with me getting hit all the time, and abused verbally, emotionally, and physically, he started hitting, screaming, and crying."

On another occasion, this human nightmare again broke into her apartment. He said he wanted to talk to her. Jennifer said, "I wanted nothing to do with him. I was so afraid. He grabbed me by my hair, turned me to face him, and punched me in my right eye. To this day, I can't see really well out of it, as it is still a little blurry. My son and another friend spending the night ran into the room, and there it was again, my son angry and terrified."

Although law enforcement was called, nothing came of it. The nightmare continued. "A couple of weeks later, I woke up to pain and about three hundred pounds of pressure on top of me. He had taped plastic gloves on his hands and was ripping me up inside. I came to find out he had raped another woman shortly before. Needless to say, I didn't press charges."

While things settled down for a while, it was too little too late for her son, who, by this time, was a very angry middle schooler. Unbeknownst to his mother, he had joined a gang. At this point, her little boy was no longer her little boy. He had so much anger and was so out of control they couldn't talk. Jennifer prayed that moving to a new house might help Joshua.

Although she still had her job at a fast-food restaurant, Jennifer said by this time she was a hardcore alcoholic. "The whiskey with my beer, come home and relax, and I didn't go anywhere without my son." As the months went on, Jennifer said she became close to a man who lived just across the street from her and Joshua. Initially, she said, David was gentle, kind, caring, and giving. Her son became good friends with him.

Eventually, David moved into their home. She remembered, "It was wonderful. The feeling in our home was very warm, and it felt blessed. The only thing that was uncomfortable was he was so jealous of everything and anything." Jennifer said she didn't know at first that David had a bad cocaine problem. When she found out and they talked about it, he told her he was doing an eight ball a day.

"I went, 'Wow,'" Jennifer said. "I couldn't believe it. But it made sense. When he was drinking beer and snorting coke, he would become extremely jealous and intimidating." The situation worsened when Jennifer discovered she had about one hundred dollars less cash than she had estimated. She asked David what happened with the missing money. His answer was not what she expected. "He slapped me so hard my ear rang. I found myself lying back with his hand around my throat. I could not breathe. For some reason, he stopped. I played it cool to be able to get out."

Jennifer walked down the stairs to her neighbor, who was cooking breakfast. "I wanted to tell her what was going on. But, of course, I knew he would come and see what was up." David did just that, and all Jennifer remembers about what happened next is a blur. When she came to, she was in her house, and the paramedics were stumbling around looking for a light switch.

She had received a terrible beating from the man she had been planning on marrying in six days. "I am pretty sure I was in total shock. To this day, I do not remember a thing, and my ear still hurts me badly."

After Jennifer's traumatic beating and emergency room trip, Joshua told her more of what had happened. It was Joshua who called the police. He told her that after the beating, David told him, "You better go check on your mom. I think I might have killed her."

And in fact, it is amazing Jennifer is still alive. She attributes that to the grace of God. She said that following the incident, "My son found part of my skull in the kitchen, crime scene and all. No child should have to go through that at any age, and for so many years." Thankfully, David is no longer a problem to her or Joshua.

It was at this point that Jennifer and Joshua lost contact for a while. They were both on the streets, but not together. Jennifer was still drinking heavily, and Joshua, understandably angry, was struggling with a gang mentality. Jennifer would quite often come into Joy Junction on an overnight basis and leave the next morning.

She said, "Before my son and I came to Joy Junction together, I came alone here and there. I couldn't find him, and he couldn't find me. It was a living nightmare. I would close my eyes and picture him shot or stabbed to death—24/7." Finally, they reestablished contact, and the two of them began coming into Joy Junction together. However, because Jennifer and Joshua were at that point staying at Joy Junction on a nightly basis, their beds were not guaranteed. On one particularly busy night for Joy Junction, they called in too late.

She said, poignantly, "We ended up behind a McDonald's dumpster downtown. Most of the time, we were together on the streets, scared and hungry. We hustled to get what we needed." It is terrifying to think what could have happened to them. Jennifer and Joshua disappeared for a while but resurfaced a few months later. A Joy Junction staff member said, "When they came back, Joshua had added some pounds and was definitely more grown-up. You could tell, though, that they had been living on the streets."

It wasn't long after this that Jennifer asked Jesus into her life. Jennifer said, "By God's will day by day we will get stronger. Joshua is my life, and with the Lord Jesus Christ, we now have a life." She is now one of the program members most of the others respect. Watching this transformation in both of them, and the resulting changes in the family unit, has been interesting and gratifying.

Thank God he had his mighty hand of protection over Jennifer, both during and after her awful abuse. I believe the Lord will continue healing the emotional scars with which Jennifer and Joshua are still dealing. And thank God for allowing us to keep the Joy Junction doors open so we can be there for the many other Jennifers and Joshuas who are out there on the streets of Albuquerque and need our help.

Amy

Amy's long and winding road to Joy Junction began fifty-nine years ago, with a grandfather who sexually abused all the girls in the family. The abuse had profound effects on Amy as she grew up. When she went through puberty, acting out with boys and men became a way of life. Amy got pregnant and initially planned on going to El Paso for an abortion. But her moral code was pro-life, and so she gave the baby up for adoption.

Amy had strict guidelines for prospective adoptive parents. They had to be Christian and involved with the community and have a military background. "I wanted my child to be safe," she said. "God, I believe, was my strength and salvation in this effort. He put me on a path where my well-intentioned goal was met. Through prayer, he gave me the strength and wisdom to find the right help as well as locate a nice family."

Amy came to Albuquerque and started working in hotels, something she did for twenty-seven years. She progressed from being a front desk clerk to working as a reservation and sales manager. But Amy was beginning a downhill emotional slide. "Depression had become a continuing problem, as well as [a] lack of trust in authority figures. I was married for seven years, and depression and anxiety led to divorce. I became increasingly isolated." She thought of ending her life.

After almost three decades of working in hotels, Amy decided a change was in order when a new company took over the hotel where she worked. She got a new job at a country club. That went well until, after eight years, sexual harassment became an issue, dredging up old, painful, and buried memories. She realized the need to face these issues and began dealing with them. As she did so, the Lord intervened. That, Amy said, "helped me to erase part of the past and start to understand God's grace."

Amy's life took another difficult turn when her mother passed away. That, she said, led to more running and a change of jobs. At that point, her son contacted her. She said that while there was a honeymoon period, "not all tales are fairy tales." She said, "I do not believe God wanted me involved in his life, long-term. He did, however, want my son to know who I was. But this is when I began to understand the dangers of trying to live up to other people's expectations. I came home again."

Amy now battled chronic depression. As a result of cuts in mental health services, the assistance she had been relying on was no longer there for her. She ended up homeless and arrived at Joy Junction one day at about four thirty in the morning. This was her first experience of homelessness, a challenging and sometimes terrifying experience for anyone. Her experience was a good one. "Everyone was very nice and helpful."

When she learned of Joy Junction's CIPP life recovery program, she joined. She thought it could help her successfully face the issues she had battled for so long. With assistance from the shelter and outside medical professionals, Amy began working on the roots of her depression and anxiety.

She said, "With the power of faith and Jesus as my Savior, I have conquered the persistent depression and running away from pain or hurt. The Lord is still teaching me to stand and accept the blessings and trials he uses to make me strong. I no longer wish to end my life. I feel that God will use me as a tool to glorify him. I can still have my feelings hurt, but the depression is no longer dark and damaging. Joy Junction cared, and through my ups and downs in the program they have continued to care. I have changed. I am not perfect, but I am continuing to change. I am born again and more joyful in life and thankful for life."

Joy Junction's Lisa Woodward said, "Even though she has graduated from the program, she still continues to help us by handing out the linens every night. Amy just can't rest unless she knows everyone has a nice area to sleep. She is part of the reason that our evenings here at Joy Junction go so well. Her gentle spirit and giving heart puts our overnight guests at ease."

Amy expects nothing and gives everything. She will tell you what a blessing Joy Junction has been to her, but she has done a lot of blessing of her own, blessing us and many of the people who are in need of our help.

Richard

I don't hold much stock in coincidences, but I am a firm believer in divinely arranged meetings. With that in mind, I regularly ask the Lord to direct my day in such a way that I will be open to where he wants me to go and open to whomever he wants me to meet. Doing so takes a lot of frustration out of difficult days and replaces it with an excitement about the next experience for me on God's agenda.

While at the Albuquerque Convention Center for our annual pre–Thanksgiving Day feast, I just "happened" to be introduced to Richard. He was there as a volunteer, helping serve hundreds of hungry people. But not so long ago, Richard was himself homeless and staying at Joy Junction. Here is some of his story.

Formerly homeless on the streets of California, Richard ended up in Albuquerque and at Joy Junction. As a result of his homelessness and other issues, he was in despair. "I was hopeless when I first got there, and Joy Junction gave me the tools I needed, such as Bible study and a little bit of hope."

Did he know Jesus? "I knew him before, but I got more intimate with him there, because I got to see that I just wasn't the only one needing help. There were more people like me. I didn't feel quite as alone. Because there were other people, as I looked around, in the same situation I'm in."

Richard said that the Bible study and the mentoring by some of our staff gave him hope and helped him the most during his stay at Joy Junction. It's been my experience that many of our guests feel pretty hopeless when they arrive, and I think it is a combination of being without a home and coping with emotionally and physically debilitating situations that land them in that sad predicament. I was so glad to hear that our staff had encouraged him.

He didn't want to say what issues specifically had landed him at Joy Junction, and I never want to press people to share anything they are not comfortable sharing. But Richard was willing to say that "hard times" in his life resulted in his homelessness. "I come from a family of nine," he said, "and we didn't have much, you know, all my life. I was in foster homes, group homes, and boys' homes, and I just had a hard time."

Good news was on the horizon. Since leaving Joy Junction, Richard now works at a local hotel, has a studio apartment, and attends a church, where he also volunteers. "I'm just giving back, because the Lord has blessed me so much."

I asked Richard what advice he would have for someone who may be in the depths of despair and is perhaps wondering if he or she could come to Joy Junction or enroll in a recovery program. Without hesitating, he said no one should stay in despair with the existence of Joy Junction and many other programs. "And don't give up, because there's a living God out there. He loves you, even if your family doesn't, if your brother doesn't, if your teacher doesn't. Jesus loves you so much."

Richard added, "I was hopeless all my life, because nobody ever loved me. I come from the projects in Los Angeles, South Central. There was no love in those projects, just drugs, alcohol, and all that stuff. But you know what? I know now that God loves me. He sent his son, Jesus Christ, to die for me. You can't get that kind of love anywhere on this earth. There's nothing else like it. You might search and search all around the world, trying to find the love in people and materialistic things, but there's no love like the love of Jesus Christ."

He encourages volunteers and donors to keep helping out, adding that doing so "makes you feel wonderful inside, and plus, we're doing the Lord's work. And that's what it's all about. Give because there are so many people out there in need, especially at Joy Junction. They take care of hundreds of women and children, so we need to give to Joy Junction."

That's what we are all about: being used as vessels so God's restorative love can be poured out spiritually and physically upon those in need.

Mike

Tall and weather-beaten with soulful eyes and a prominent moustache, Mike was a hard person to miss. I met him at a citywide Crusade for the Homeless, where a number of relief agencies were gathered for the day as a sort of "one-stop shop" for the homeless. Services offered included haircuts, food, clothing, and an array of information to make the lives of the homeless and near-homeless a little easier.

Mike stopped by our booth, and I asked him to tell me some of his story. He said he has a home and he is grateful for it. But it is difficult, as the assistance check that pays his rent is the only thing that is guaranteed. For Mike, everything else is a mass of uncertainty, "not knowing from month to month whether I'm going to be able to pay my utilities and keep those on. And supply myself with food. Sometimes I can get assistance, and other times not."

Not knowing where your next meal is going to come from is no way to live—"especially when you have health problems and health issues, and there are some foods that you can't really eat, because it'll make your health issues worse."

I asked Mike if he thought that people he encounters really understand the plight faced by those in his condition. He said the majority of them don't. "They ask you questions. You start telling them the truth about something, and they'll turn around and walk away." He said, "It kinda makes me feel useless, like I don't have a place anymore in this world, in this economy. I used to have a very good job, and it's very difficult these days with the economy and with jobs that have been outsourced to other countries—especially manufacturing, which is what I was doing for over twenty years."

Events like the Crusade for the Homeless are very important to people like Mike. "Today, I'm here looking for clothes for the winter. If it wasn't for something like this, and other places like it, there wouldn't be anything."

How would Mike respond to those who say that if he wanted to he could do more on his own? He said, "Those people don't really understand, because not everybody on the street or close to being without a home are addicted people. There are people like me that have gotten caught up in this in this economy, too." He hopes they won't dismiss everyone they see on the streets with a backpack as being addicts unable to get a job.

I echo Mike's words, but I would expand on them to say we are also obligated to show the love of Jesus to addicts. It is so easy for us to label people as incorrigible and make off-the-cuff judgmental statements and say (maybe a tad smugly), "If that was me, I wouldn't be in that position." The point is that the person about whom we are commenting is not us, and there but for the grace of God go you and I. Many times we have no idea what led the addict (who we sometimes blithely dismiss and depersonalize as "that junkie") to end up in his or her predicament.

I am not defending a person's use of illegal drugs. Absolutely not. But prayerfully consider circumstances such as abuse, rejection, rape, or mental illness that may have resulted in, or contributed to, a drug user's difficult position. The next time someone asks you for help, would you prayerfully consider your specific role as a Good Samaritan for the needy? What you decide could potentially determine the physical and spiritual destiny of a homeless or needy person in Albuquerque, or in whichever city you live.

If you are like me, I know you do not want to make anyone feel useless and without a place in the world.

Doug

The emotionally and physically worn man was sitting in his van with a sign in the window reading Homeless Vet Needs Work. As I looked at him, I wondered what he had experienced. His face suggested he was tired and perhaps somewhat desperate. Beyond that, there wasn't that much more visibly apparent. He appeared to exhibit a quite understandable guard.

The van was parked outside a Whole Foods Market, a few miles from Albuquerque's downtown. As I walked over to the van to see if I could help, a small dog growled and barked protectively. I introduced myself and asked the occupant whether I could help and if he would tell me his story. His name was Doug.

Doug told me he came to Albuquerque during the winter, en route to Long Beach, California, and ended up getting stuck in Albuquerque. More specifically, he had car problems and ran out of money. And with a job awaiting him in Kansas City, he was anxious to be on his way.

I asked Doug how receptive people were to his plight, and he said they had been pretty nice, but I inferred he had experienced a pretty difficult time in obtaining employment. In fact, he said getting a job could be easier said than done. "Not everybody has a pristine past. Some people have a checkered past. They made mistakes, and just because you go in front of a court and they give you a sentence, it doesn't stop there. It follows you. So a lot of times you fill out an application, and you don't tell them about your past. Then once they get on the computer, they find out about it, or you tell them about it, and you don't get a job. So it's kind of a catch-22."

Shannon was Doug's dog. "I was camped out by the American Legion on Lomas. I sleep with the doors open, and I woke up one morning, and she was in my driver's seat. I tried to get her to move, and she bit me. We have been together ever since. Yeah, she bites me every day, but she's my buddy."

Doug told me he thinks using some federal stimulus money to help the homeless would be great thing to do to put more people to work who would otherwise be a drain on society. I asked him where he would spend that night. He said probably by the American Legion on Lomas. He felt that location was safe because of the close presence of the legion. In addition to that, there were very few people there, so he felt safe sleeping with the doors open.

What would it be like sleeping outside in what could be such potentially dangerous conditions? What if the weather went from cold to freezing? Would Doug survive the night? What if bugs started crawling over his body? Would he even be able to sleep? Even though he believes he will be safe, what if he were harassed? Would he make it out alive? Would his adrenaline keep him going? Would a fight-or-flight reaction kick in?

Posttraumatic stress disorder makes it difficult for Doug to stay at homeless shelters, as that usually means being around and getting along with a lot of other people. He said while he would take donations to help him along the way, he was also willing to work. I bought Doug some gas and some food to help him on his way. I prayed and wished him Godspeed.

My mind was in overdrive as I drove home that night. What has gone wrong with our country when someone like Doug, a veteran, slowly and perilously makes his way from city to city? Would he ever make it to his new job in Kansas City? I knew I would make it to my final destination. I knew the comforts that awaited me when I arrived home. But what about Doug? What would it take to help get him to his destination? And how long would that take?

I only know the answers can be found in the hands of God and in those he prompted to help Doug. (Kathy Sotelo contributed to this story.)

Debbie

Debbie enjoyed a good childhood. She was raised in a Christian home and attended Christian schools. But all that was to change when she turned fifteen. Debbie said, "My innocence was taken away by a rape that ended up being an unwanted pregnancy. Being an adopted child, I put my daughter up for adoption to Christian parents. The pain was too great for me to handle."

Reaction of Christians to the incident hurt Debbie. She also began questioning how the Lord could allow one of his children to be harmed in such a manner. As a result, she started running from her family and other loved ones, and for years, she kept running. And as she ran from the Lord, she wound up in the arms of the Enemy.

She said, "I ran to drugs, and this led to men who were abusive mentally, physically, and sexually. It seemed like I could not get away from this type of lifestyle." Debbie said she finally decided to settle down, get married, and raise a family, thinking her life would change. But it didn't. There was always some kind of abuse from her husband. "I left my husband and three children, returning to my old lifestyle in the dark world of alcohol, drugs, and bikers." The second man Debbie married was a biker, and once again, she had entered into an abusive relationship. She became his "property." The second marriage soon ended in a violent divorce, and Debbie was homeless for a time. Her next relationship turned out to be one of more unkept promises. It ended when she was again addicted to drugs and, as she put it, tired of being "broken."

She wanted to find out who she was really destined to be. She knew the answer in her heart but felt she had strayed from that place. In an attempt to fix the damage, Debbie found herself at the women's division of a gospel mission. She was addicted to pain pills, crack, and marijuana. A staff member suggested she sign up for the mission's rehab program, Family Hope Discipleship, and Debbie did not hesitate. "I wanted change. I needed to let go and let God do his work in me. About one month later, at a huge church, I accepted Christ back into my life." Two weeks after that, she was rebaptized in one of the nearby lakes with about eighty other people. "Wow! What an amazing, warm feeling came over me when I came up from the water. I knew the Spirit was in me."

Debbie did well until she fell in love with a man from the men's discipleship program. After eight months, the two of them were asked to leave. She and her boyfriend did very well for a while, but that was about to change. She said, "Soon, he began to drink, and things started to go down real fast from there." Not long after, Debbie's boyfriend was diagnosed with third-stage small cell lung cancer. She said, "My faith soared during this time, despite his illness. I quit my job to take care of him full-time. He had become paralyzed, and his speech was slurred. God answered our prayers during this time. Our best friend finally told him, 'You should marry Debbie. She has gone through so much for you.'"

The two of them got married, and their church raised enough money for his ex-wife and daughter to fly in from Grants, New Mexico, for the wedding. After ten years, he would see his only daughter. "A miracle," Debbie said. "Just 168 hours later, my husband died in his sleep. I never lost faith during this whole time, even though I was mad at God for taking him from me." Debbie said in the last three weeks of her husband's life, God brought them back to the gospel mission to be around the friends and teachers they had in rehab. She stayed there for eight months.

Debbie and her teenage daughter then went to live with her oldest daughter. She stayed single and didn't date for sixteen months. She texted an old friend named Allen the words "Happy New Year," and a friendship between her and Allen started to bloom.

She lost her job and could not save her house. Due to stress, she found herself in the hospital, while the courts put a twenty-four-hour quit notice on the house. She lost everything. Debbie was homeless again. That resulted in Debbie and Allen staying with friends for a few weeks.

Meanwhile, Allen decided to turn himself in for an old DUI in a nearby county. Debbie returned to the mission once again, leaving every morning to go to work, while her teenage daughter was going to a friend's house and running the streets. After Allen was released, their troubles increased. They stayed in a rundown hotel in Kalamazoo for about a month. As a result of some bad associations, they received death threats. Debbie said, "The threats kept coming, and I started having nightmares of Allen being shot in front of me and dying in my arms." Despite the threats, Debbie said their faith kept them strong, and they grew closer. Allen's uncle lived in Tijeras, New Mexico, and he told them to come out. They loaded up their car with all their belongings and headed west.

Things went well for a while. While in Tijeras, Allen spent his mornings chopping wood and talking to God while Debbie read Psalms and Proverbs, and then they would both write to God. "I really felt closer to God being in the mountains."

But they left Allen's uncle's place and came to Joy Junction. "Since being here, we have told people our story and shared with them what God has done with us. We have tried every day to serve God in all we have done here. Though we have our ups and downs, we do not lose our focus on God."

Where would Debbie and Allen have gone without Joy Junction? Debbie said, "We would have had nowhere to go without Joy Junction; home was not an option. To me, this is a safe haven for myself and for people who are broken in any area of their lives. Here they can find healing. No matter why I'm here, God has been with me. He has never left me, and he never will." Debbie added, "I feel more comfortable, and my walk is getting stronger every day. My heart is turning into a servant's heart, with no questions of why."

Debbie and Allen have always stepped up to help other members of the Joy Junction community in need. They do this with a nonjudgmental, humble attitude. What a blessing it is for us to be involved with them and in the lives of all the guests the Lord brings to our doors.

Robert

Even die-hard chili lovers may not be so grateful if all they got for Christmas was a bowl of chili. But Robert was delighted. Homeless, he sat outside a fast-food restaurant on Albuquerque's Ninety-Eighth Street on a wind-chilled Christmas Eve. We were dispensing some Christmas cheer from our Lifeline of Hope food wagon. Among other things, we were giving chili, soup, sack lunches, coffee, soft drinks, blankets, and personal hygiene kits.

The wind whipped through my bones as I stood there talking to Robert. I asked him how the chili made him feel. Robert replied, "It makes me feel great. It makes me feel very happy. No one else has given me anything for Christmas. I'm just happy you guys are here."

He told me something about his plight. He had been living in a shed with an electric heater close to the restaurant for about six weeks. Before that, he had been living on the streets. Robert described the difficulties of living outside. "It was pretty cold in the winter. I didn't have blankets or anything. Sometimes, all I had was my jacket to cover myself. It was pretty cold at night, and it was pretty cold in the mornings. I'd get up in the mornings and wonder what I was going to make my breakfast with. Sometimes, I'd go over to one of the shelters, and they were all filled up, and they'd have no room to put me up for the night. So, I had to sleep on the street."

What caused Robert to become homeless? He said the deaths of his whole family precipitated his descent into homelessness just two years before. "I have no one. I used to have my mother to go to. She'd put me up for the night, for the evening, or I'd go to one of my brothers.

They're all gone ... My aunts, my uncles—my whole family's gone. My grandmother's gone, my grandfather's gone, my cousins—they're all gone. They all passed away."

Robert said it's hard to get through each day. "Sometimes, I come over here [to the fast-food restaurant] in the morning and drink coffee. If I'm lucky, somebody will ask me, 'Have you eaten yet?' They'll buy me maybe a hamburger or something to eat in the morning. But in the afternoon, you've got to try to make a little bit of change or something. Then I get a loaf of bread or something, or a little bag of bologna to take home."

He said his faith helped him make it through each day. "I pray every night and every morning when I wake up. I thank the good Lord for helping me make it through the night and helping me make it through the day. I pray to him every day." Robert's hopes for the New Year were very modest and practical. His doctor wanted to operate on his knee. "If they operate on my knee, then hopefully I can find a little janitorial work, as a custodian or something, that doesn't have heavy lifting. Hopefully, then I'll get a place to live."

But Robert had more medical troubles than just his knee. He had what looked like serious frostbite on the back of his right hand and right index finger. He promised me he would get some medical attention immediately following the Christmas holidays.

To those of our donors who made our Christmas Eve trip of cheer possible, Robert has this to say: "Just never lose hope; keep on praying, and Jesus will come through one way or another. The people at Joy Junction—they're beautiful. They come out here and feed you, and whenever you're feeling down, they help you the best way they know how."

Robert's optimism is absolutely phenomenal. He doesn't have a place to stay, yet he was encouraging us to have hope and faith. What a lesson for those of us who have so much and still find ourselves wanting more.

Carrie

Here's another one of those "coincidences" I believe are really divine appointments. While leaving a diner on Central (Route 66), close to some of Albuquerque's homeless hot spots, after a late working lunch, Joy Junction's Kathy Sotelo and I were stopped by a well-dressed woman. Carrie apologized for what she called an "intrusion" and asked me if I was Jeremy Reynalds from the homeless shelter. When I told her I was, she nervously asked me if we could possibly buy her a meal. I quickly said yes. She was obviously embarrassed and close to tears.

Carrie told us she had been employed by a local corporation but had been laid off and was unable to find a new job. She had run through all her savings and didn't know what to do. She said she hadn't eaten at all the day we met her.

I asked Carrie if she still had a place to stay. She said she paid her rent and telephone bill three months in advance and was determined not to live on the streets. However, eating was a different matter. Like too many people in these hard economic days in America, she had to make a choice between paying the rent and having food to eat.

Kathy gave her numbers for some local resources, and I asked her if we could pray for her. She graciously agreed, so we joined hands, and for just a brief moment, we turned that diner into a holy place. When we opened our eyes, Carrie's eyes were moist, and she hugged us both. What was the "chance" of Carrie passing the diner at the exact moment we were coming out? I believe it was a divinely arranged meeting.

Route 66 is somewhere the Lord Jesus Christ—his love, presence, and Spirit—is very much alive and active.

Melissa

Melissa says that the worst part of being homeless is "when you have to go without food—and when it's just so cold that you can't even bear it, and you don't have enough to wrap up in, and you're losing feeling in your body parts because you're so cold." She is a missionary pastor's daughter and didn't plan to be virtually homeless, living with her husband on the West Mesa in Albuquerque, New Mexico. But that is how she started 2010.

I met Melissa recently while on an outreach with the Joy Junction Lifeline of Hope food wagon. She told me how appreciative she was of the supplies we had given her and her husband. She called the unexpected gifts "wonderful."

Melissa's life is very difficult due to ongoing pain, a number of surgeries, and a delayed disability assessment. While living in Chicago and working in the medical field, she dislocated her shoulders, tore up her hand, hit her nose, and had to have reconstructive sinus and hand surgery. Now in Albuquerque as a result of her husband's employment, Melissa is undergoing a series of operations.

After Melissa's husband left his job, he began traveling and looking for employment. Ultimately, he found work in Albuquerque, but it hasn't been at all easy. There are a lot of barriers to moving into an apartment or a house that people don't necessarily think about, Melissa said. "I don't even know my way around Albuquerque. I don't know the good places or the bad ones. How am I going to feel like I'm safe to go off and get an apartment when I don't even know the area?"

Fortunately, she has been able to communicate. "My family bought me a cell phone, and they pay for it so that I can at least get all my doctors' calls. Between that, you know, and them helping me, that's all I get. My unemployment's all gone, and they wouldn't even let me have an extension. They told me I didn't make enough to get an extension."

Melissa said the people of Albuquerque have treated her wonderfully. "So much more wonderful than Chicago, where I'm from. I think that's one thing that keeps me out here." To the people who have helped her, such as her husband's employer, she says, "Thank you to everybody who pulled together during the times when I needed it. I didn't have a vehicle when I went in for surgery, so my husband's boss he let him take me to surgery in the service truck. He picked me up in the service truck and gets my medicine in the service truck. There are good people out here."

Melissa is also grateful for the Joy Junction donors, whose kindness and generosity allows us to keep the Lifeline of Hope on the road. She said if it weren't for the Lifeline, she would have to wait another month before being able to buy desperately needed supplies. Not having the needed food and supplies is the most difficult thing about being homeless. And at that point, Melissa said, "I feel like I'm alone ... and that nobody cares." But I reminded her, "We care for you, Jesus cares for you, and a lot of generous donors around town care for you as well."

I asked Melissa what hopes she has for the upcoming year. She said she wants to make it through the remainder of her six surgeries and get her disability. "I don't want to be pushed away by the courts any longer because of my age. I'm hurt, and I can't work ever again, even if the surgeries do work."

Melissa said her relationship with Jesus enabled her to get through the last year. She said, "Without him, I wouldn't be here. I would have already committed suicide. I can guarantee you that. I have been through such a hard last fifteen months that if it wasn't for the Lord, I would have just said, 'Forget it.'" She encourages everyone who reads her story to believe in God. "If you do, he'll bring you the good people, and that means really believing in God when you're down and out, crying to him. Don't cry to your mom. You really, really have to 100 percent believe, and people will come to you. They will be there to help."

Melissa is one of the flock God allows us to reach. It is such a great opportunity to share the love of Jesus Christ tangibly with those who are outside the walls of Joy Junction. Our friends and donors make it possible.

William

Traveling the streets of Albuquerque on Joy Junction's Lifeline of Hope meal wagon provides an opportunity to share the spiritual and physical love of Jesus with people the Lord chooses to put in our way. It is such a blessing to share food and essential supplies to worried and discouraged people.

Some of these people were involuntarily displaced from an apartment complex that had been closed by the city as substandard. We passed a man with a sign, sitting on the corner of Menaul and Carlisle. He had eyes of heartfelt desperation. It was as if they bore into our souls and compelled us to stop. We pulled into a parking lot, introduced ourselves, and asked the man if he was hungry. He said he was, so we gave him a sack lunch and a bottle of vitamin water. He asked for another lunch and water for his friend, which we happily gave. We gave another sack lunch to a man who asked for an extra meal for his friend "who can't get up and come over here." Again, we were happy to oblige. We have found it a common occurrence that many of the homeless are very concerned for their friends and that there is an intense camaraderie between those in need.

Then there's William, who we met at another location where we feed people. He told me that the Lifeline helps a lot. "Because when I don't got nothing, they always come help me right here. Always," he said.

William told me a bit of his story, and he had some pretty good advice about the perils of drinking. He said, "I used to drink hard liquor every day—vodka, whiskey, anything I could get. It almost caused me to lose my family and everything. My wife told me to choose the alcohol or choose my family. I choose my family. I still drink a bit every now and then, but it's nothing like being an alcoholic. At least I'm doing better. I'm getting better at it, and I'm still with my wife for thirty years."

Faith is how William has gotten through all the trials in his life. "Faith. Faith in my Lord Jesus Christ, and my wife being on my side. She keeps my best part of me. She makes a difference in me doing better." William had experienced some tough love from his wife, of whom he spoke so admiringly. She told him, "'You either want me and the kids, or you want to live by yourself and be homeless.' I didn't want to be homeless; I love my wife and my kids." As a result, William said, he decided to put his wife and family ahead of alcohol. He continued, "I put them first from now on in my life because God blessed me … and gave me the strength to do so."

What would William say to those thinking of experimenting with alcohol or drugs? "That's not a good thing. You need to recognize it is okay to drink a little bit occasionally, but not to be a drunk. Never be a drunk."

I asked William what he sees ahead. He said, "God blessing everybody through my Lord Jesus Christ. Keep your faith in the Lord Jesus Christ, and you'll be all right." William, I couldn't say it better. Thanks for brightening our day when we see you in your part of Albuquerque. I pray you keep serving the Lord and grow in his grace and love.

A Slice of Life at Joy Junction

Have you ever wondered about life behind the scenes at a homeless shelter? I don't mean what you get to see on those special "open house" days, when the shelter puts its proverbial best foot forward. I am talking about typical everyday life.

I spent some time observing a slice of life at Joy Junction, and I have written about this in my book *Homeless Culture and the Media*. For continuity of the story, I have condensed the observation times into a couple of days, when they were in fact longer.

A Sunday Afternoon

It is three twenty on a relatively calm Sunday afternoon in the main building of Joy Junction. A pregnant guest, holding a baby, is distraught about the recent abandonment of five children at Joy Junction; the kids ended up being placed in foster care. She says, "I just want to go out and find that woman. But my husband says, 'Maybe she was suicidal, so perhaps the kids are in a better place.'" I ponder briefly their vastly different reactions to the abandonment.

A man with physical and mental problems staggers into the office and says, "I hate channel four," Someone asks him why, and he replies, "Because they always cut out."

Just as the channel four hater is wobbling out, a Joy Junction staffer comes in. He is casually dressed in a plaid shirt with a blue undershirt and blue jeans, and his hair is sticking up. He asks the shelter pastor, "That girl you had at the movies. Was she eighteen?"

"No, she was in her midfifties," responds the pastor.

"Okay, just trying to scare you," says the Joy Junction parking lot attendant. That's typical humor at Joy Junction. I've heard that humor like this is a coping mechanism that often shows up in environments like ours.

A few minutes later, I hear a snippet of a sad conversation drifting out of a neighboring office. "He drinks too much, and he's already hit her."

It is now four thirty, and dinner is well under way. Most people are sitting and eating their evening meal, but about a dozen or so are still standing in the serving line. There is not much audible conversation going on from my fairly unobtrusive listening post a few feet away, just a few laughs here and there.

I can only see one person not eating, an elderly black woman with graying hair, sitting quietly on a couch. Her vacant stare personifies the stereotypical image many people have of the homeless.

A Well-Ordered Atmosphere

The overall atmosphere behind the scenes at Joy Junction resembles a busy, well-ordered, and well-structured beehive. While it appears (to me, anyway) to be a comforting, reassuring environment, I wonder how many of the scores of people I can see eating dinner are as comfortable with it as I am. Maybe my comfort level is due at least in part to my being the director and my having been here so long. Also, I am not homeless; they are.

By 5:10, supper is over, and all the tables have been stacked to one side to make way for the upcoming church service. As a faith-based ministry, church services and Bible studies form a core part of Joy Junction's mission.

I hear another snatch of conversation coming out of an office. Someone says, "All you had to do was answer the question." Another person says, "Tough it out." The first individual responds, "I'm tired."

A couple of minutes later, two tall men begin their after-dinner chores of methodically sweeping and mopping the floor prior to the chairs being put back down for church. Daily chores are required as a condition for staying at the shelter. Continued refusal to do chores will eventually result in the individual being asked to leave. It's all about trying to help our guests be responsible and transition back into the real world.

The black woman is still sitting in the same place. The only difference is that she now has a soft-covered Bible balanced on her lap. There are about a dozen people sitting on the couches that line the perimeter of the building. They are all just looking.

Later, a kitchen worker drops off some meals for the workers on an upcoming shift. He is a troubled but affable young man who needs some positive male role models in his life. I ask him if he's behaving. He says, "Yeah, I was just dropping off lunches. See, I've stacked them nice and neat." He knows who I am, and he is anxious to please.

The kitchen worker disappears from sight, but then a man comes by and stops at the office right in front of my listening post. I ask him how he's doing. He says, "Not so good." I ask him why, and he replies that because he has broken up with his spouse, his stay at Joy Junction has now reverted to overnight status. He's disappointed and says, "I had a lot of plans. I had a lot I could do for this place. See these three couches? That's what I used to do for my business. I used to fix them." I utter condolences, saying, "Yeah, that's what happens."

He responds, "Rules are rules," and walks off. This is the man who has been accused by his wife of hitting her. Even though I've now worked with the homeless for over twenty years and think there is nothing left to surprise me, some things still do. This man is apparently more concerned about his inability to fix the shelter's couches than he is about his relationship with his wife.

People continue to sit.

At 5:35, with the chores completed, the sound service is in the final stages of set up, and the chairs are being put back on the floor for the 6:00 church service.

At 5:40, the band is practicing. A handful of people are sitting in the bright orange and yellow chairs, waiting for the service to begin. A smiling African American woman waves to me and points proudly to the baby she has cradled in her lap. The pastor is making some last-minute adjustments to the sound system, and a number of people are sitting around on couches.

It's now 6:00, and guests are singing, "Sing a joyful song unto the Lord. Praise the Lord with gladness because he alone is God."

There is a small amount of clapping going on to accompany the singing. Seventeen people are standing up, about 15 percent of the entire crowd. While most of those singing don't have a home, they still want to sing and worship the Lord. It is spiritual hope in the midst of physical despair. I realize that a similar scene is duplicated in hundreds of gospel rescue missions across the country.

While the singing is under way, a man supported by a walker at the back of the building stands, looking on. Just behind him in the building entrance is a shopping cart piled high with clean bed linens ready to be put away. There is a stark contrast between the normal church service at the front of the building and a normal homeless scene at the back.

Monday Morning

At 7:55, I am back at my vantage point in the office of Joy Junction's main building. It is very quiet, with just a couple of people sitting around on chairs.

A woman approaches and says, "I was in bed for thirty days with the flu. My doctor years ago in Arkansas gave me a little blue pill, which had no side effects. I had to take it every day. It was just an allergy tablet. It's allergies. I was just born with that reaction. Some of the people here really don't care. Their brains still race. I just wanna get rid of these sinus sniffles. It's been an infection."

She stops for a moment, and I look across the building to where a man is doing his morning chores, slowly and methodically mopping the floor. Chores are always on the agenda at a shelter the size of ours.

The woman continues talking and says, "Spanish people, they talk so fast. *'Amigo, amigo.'* Four years of it. I beg their pardon. You think they talk slow. They don't."

She suddenly switches gears and blurts out, "You ever been down to 'La Jumbo Fish,' crawfish pie? Why is it so important to remember the names of songs these days?"

The woman wanders off but returns quickly with a purposeful walk and says, "Did they ever cure whiplash? I was in a vehicle accident in east Texas. I was a passenger and impacted by an eighteen-wheeler. What do you have to do to get a neck brace? Go in the ER?" She puts her hand on the back of her neck and wanders off again.

I realize that while she is apparently seriously mentally ill, I have nonetheless heard much worse during my years spent working with New Mexico's homeless.

A Quiet Interlude

At 9:40, it is still very quiet. A couple of boys are walking around aimlessly. One of them is swinging a pair of socks. Four people are sitting at the table, talking. A lady is sitting on a couch, apparently engrossed in something, although it may be nothing. I hear snippets of conversation from a neighboring office. A voice says, "Michael is going to be upset when he gets home."

Someone responds, "I seem to have no eyesight when I first wake up. I just can't find it." I love Joy Junction humor. My staff says a lot of it is my fault.

I am startled out of my brief reverie when an unknown guest appears in front of me and says, "Hi, Jeremy. I didn't know you were Jeremy." She walks off without saying anything else.

There are now six people in the multipurpose room. A woman is sitting on the couch with her suitcase in front of her.

At one o'clock in the afternoon the suitcase lady is still sitting on the couch. An elderly-looking woman, who I suspect is much younger than she looks, comes to the office door and looks at me but talks to herself. She then puts her hand on her stomach and moves away.

It is quiet at 3:35. I can see five people.

At 4:15, a woman calls and asks if she and her three children can come to the shelter. She and her husband stayed with us some years ago. They committed their lives to the Lord, and we thought they were doing well. I learn that her husband quit his job against the advice of his pastor and wife, and instead of looking for another job, he has been reading the Bible and spending all his time consumed in Bible prophecy.

The wife says the situation has become too much for her to handle, and when she told her husband to get a job, he starting hitting her. Not surprisingly, she left. As the woman is checking into the shelter, I hear her gratefully exclaim, "Thank God that at least we've got a place to stay!" "Where?" asks the youngest of her three children. "Right here," says Mom, pointing to a couch before they were given a room. "Weird," says the little girl, clutching a donated stuffed animal. "Very weird." Out of the mouth of babes.

It is 5:07 p.m., and supper is being held up briefly, as all the volunteers coming to serve are not here yet. There are about twenty-five people sitting around, some at tables and some on couches.

Dinnertime

At 5:22, everyone is quietly seated at tables, waiting to be served by the volunteers, who have now all arrived. The exception to the quiet is a baby crying in its mother's arms.

It is 8:10, and the building is full of people getting ready to go to bed. People are lying on mattresses and couches all around the building.

At 8:20, a young child is running around. I hear someone asking for a toothbrush. Our driver comes in, clutching a donation of eight dozen maple donuts—a staple for shelters. He asks for a key to the kitchen.

A couple of minutes later, a former guest thanks me for helping her out again. She is in Albuquerque only for the night so she can bail her husband out of jail for public drunkenness. She says, "I miss this place. That's why I'm volunteering tonight." She doesn't tell me just exactly what it is she is volunteering to do.

At 8:55, a woman comes into the office to talk to the women's counselor, who is doing double duty answering the telephones. The woman has been written up for being "disruptive" during the previous night's church service, and she is very annoyed. She says she wasn't at all disruptive but had been laughing at a funny comment the pastor made.

At 8:58, a loudly crying child has interrupted the quiet hum.

At 9:01, the lights should be out, but things are running a little late. Most people are now lying on their beds, talking or reading. I see one man sitting on his mattress fiddling with a roll of toilet paper and a woman sitting on her mattress drearily combing out her hair.

It is now 9:04, and the lights are turned out in the multipurpose building. Lights are turned out in common areas at 9:00 and at 10:00 in private rooms. It is almost the end of another day at Joy Junction.

God in the Details: Everyday Evidence around Joy Junction

Pointing to a small baseball bat positioned close to him on the counter, the bat-toting businessman said he used it to threaten and chase away any homeless people coming in his store who he perceived as being troublesome.

I could scarcely believe what I was hearing. Joy Junction's Kathy Sotelo and I were on a Friday outreach in Joy Junction's Lifeline of Hope food wagon. During one of our stops, we met Peter, a man we'd been helping, who asked us if we would stop by an area liquor store to talk to the owner. Peter said the owner had been experiencing problems with homeless people, prostitutes, and drug addicts.

We said we would be glad to. We've visited many places and left our business cards, which display an 800 number people can call any time of the day or night for the homeless to get a ride to Joy Junction. We parked by the heavily barred and fortified store and made our way into what could be described as an alcoholic's paradise. A buzzer alerted store employees to our entrance.

Kathy spoke first to the individual at the counter. She introduced us and gave the man our cards and a Joy Junction brochure. He turned out to be the business owner. She explained our van service to Joy Junction and how that could help him assist individuals hanging around his store in need of shelter and other assistance.

Without hesitation, the store owner told us he did not have a problem with the homeless. He said he would just "take a baseball bat to 'em."

As we exited the store in complete shock, Kathy said, "His helping the people in need around here wouldn't be good for business." Without her saying any more, I knew what she meant. Like her, I suspected that this angry man was only too willing to serve the homeless when they had money to give him for the alcohol that would feed their life-controlling addiction. But when they were out of cash and every pore of their body still cried out for alcohol, they were out of luck. Pathetic. This man was not even willing to call Joy Junction.

My mind started whirling, trying to anticipate some of the questions I knew would be asked if I told this story. I suspected the main one would be "Isn't this man is a businessman trying to make an honest living? People don't have to drink, right?"

Wrong! Obviously, the initial choice was theirs, but who knows what circumstances these precious souls were navigating that caused them to drown their sorrows in a blurry alcoholic haze? And it didn't take very long before that initial bad choice (and who among us hasn't made a series of bad choices?) became a life-controlling addiction.

Kathy and I got back in the Lifeline of Hope wagon, and I turned the key. Nothing happened. I tried again, but all we heard was a click. I guessed it was an ignition problem, or maybe it was the battery or alternator. "Oh, well," I told Kathy, "the Lord has a reason for this." Admittedly, at that point I had no idea what it was. We called Robert Batrez, our staff mechanic at Joy Junction. He said he would be there as soon as he could, so we settled back to wait.

We were sitting in the food wagon when Peter approached us, and he was concerned when we couldn't get the wagon to start. As we waited for Robert to come to our assistance, I told Peter about our experience in the liquor store. He said, "He [the store owner] gets them addicted and then profits from their addictions."

Robert arrived and got under the hood to work out why the Lifeline of Hope wouldn't start. Nothing seemed to work until Peter leaned on the food wagon. Call it a miracle or divine intervention, but as soon as he touched the truck, it started! We were once again shocked! What was it about Peter? As soon as the Lifeline was running, Peter, who knew the area, rounded up a variety of people in need, and we prayed with some of them and provided chili, soup, sack lunches, and personal hygiene kits. We fed about thirty people, precious souls who would have otherwise gone to bed that night with hunger pangs gnawing at their stomachs.

I was trying to understand what had occurred when the Lord assured me the incident was not about Peter. Rather, it was all about Jesus! He wanted us to encourage some discouraged folk in this terribly economically depressed part of Albuquerque. He used Peter and a temporarily disabled Lifeline of Hope truck to communicate his will to us.

And he uses our supporters and donors to do the same thing, because they make it possible for Joy Junction to accomplish its ongoing ministry of compassion.

A Heartwarming Christmas Tale

The day before Christmas Eve was an even busier one than usual for the Joy Junction staff. Our mission, which is home to as many as three hundred people, including as many as eighty children, was abuzz with pre-Christmas excitement. The youngsters were very excited, like all children at this season. At least for a while, they were able to forget their homelessness and anxiously anticipate a multitude of gifts made possible by generous donors. The volunteers unloaded bags of Santa's treasures, and the children followed their parents' instruction to "open just one present today." Parents mumble that they have no idea where they will put it all.

However, falling snowflakes diverted the children's attention. They came running to Joy Junction's Lisa Woodward, asking her, "Can you call Dr. Reynolds? Please, Lees" (the children's affectionate name for her). Lisa was curious why the youngsters wanted her to call me. She tried explaining that I was very busy.

The kids insisted. "Ask him if we can build a snowman." "Does he like snowball fights?" "Will he let [kitchen manager] Mike make us snow ice cream?" Lisa laughed and promised them she would e-mail their requests to my ever-active BlackBerry and return with an answer should we actually get enough snow to scoop up.

This was not what the kids wanted to hear. Lisa said, "Slightly annoyed with my apparent lack of being able to prioritize, they wandered off with a parting comment, 'Lees, you better remember. We are gonna ask him. He likes us.'" She watched the children make their way to a Christmas activity and reminded them about the true meaning of Christmas and why we give gifts. She was touched when she heard the kids talk about how the Lord would understand their dilemma and phone the good Dr. Reynalds.

Lisa said, "I remember flashes of my Christmases prior to Joy Junction. But I never felt love or the true spirit of Christmas until I came here." Lisa, who lives on-site, said, "Someday I will live in a dwelling away from the loving land of Joy Junction. Who knew that this ground could be so blessed or beautiful? But I hope God will call Dr. Reynalds every year and remind him to invite me home for the holidays."

I appreciate the tireless efforts of Lisa and the rest of our staff. Working at Joy Junction is so much more than a job. It is a calling. We must thank our Lord for his faithfulness, and we must thank our donors for supporting us. Without them, we could not share the love of Jesus with the ever-increasing number of people in need.

The Disappearing Diapers:
A Higher Street Value than Cocaine

During the Thanksgiving and Christmas seasons, Joy Junction is blessed with an outpouring of donations of toys, food, clothing, personal hygiene kits, and more.

One Christmas season, we had an organization donate cases and cases of diapers. While diapers may seem a pretty mundane gift to most of us, it is hard to appreciate their value until they are needed and not available. As a result, the families staying at Joy Junction felt as if Christmas had arrived early.

As things settled down (at least until the next kindhearted group of generous donors came by), Joy Junction's Lisa Woodward told me she learned that a few of the shelter's single residents had taken several cases of the donated diapers. Quite understandably, she was more than a little curious and started an immediate search. We shelter between sixty and eighty children nightly with their parents, so diapers donated to Joy Junction are a precious commodity.

Lisa found out that a few of the individuals who had taken the diapers had children living off-site with family members or friends. While she was not thrilled to learn they had taken the diapers without going through the proper channels, she did understand. After all, how must these mothers feel when told by their children's caregivers that diapers are a badly needed but perhaps financially unattainable item?

But Lisa found out something else that floored her. She asked one of the residents why she had two bundles of diapers. The woman asked Lisa if she worked for Joy Junction and if she was not aware of some of the informational releases put out by the shelter. Lisa said, "I was fairly sure I was aware of most of the releases, but in this age of Facebook and Twitter, maybe I was not aware of everything." The resident told Lisa that her boss (me) was aware that there are minimal toilet facilities in downtown Albuquerque for the homeless, and that situation puts the homeless in a humiliating dilemma. She said that because of the lack of toilets, the homeless have to disgrace themselves by urinating and defecating behind dumpsters and any other place with some privacy. It is doubly bad for females, as they must disrobe to do either.

This resident told Lisa that when she and other homeless individuals could not make it to a day shelter or Joy Junction, they could use the diapers in their jeans and then discard the waste with some dignity. She stated that diapers had a better street value than cocaine. Lisa said, "I was stopped in my tracks. I have been homeless, and I have worked within the gates of Joy Junction for a little over four years. But I had never heard this. I apologized to the resident for questioning her and returned to my office very humbled."

The lack of restrooms is a big problem, and so the homeless have learned to be creative. These residents said the downtown Albuquerque library and the Alvarado Transportation Center were their first and second choices, respectively. One individual said you have to be "sneaky" when using the Greyhound terminal. He only uses it when he has enough time and money to pretend he is getting a snack or looking at schedules. Even then, he said, once you leave, he had to make sure to disappear and not hang out in front.

Some homeless people hop over fences on construction sites and use the portable toilets there. At other times, they will just "find a spot." Some Joy Junction guests say when they ask for directions to a restroom, many times they are either ignored or receive hateful responses. One person was told, "If you had a home, you would know where the bathroom is." A comment like this is so hateful it defies description.

At Joy Junction, we remember the plight of those who have no home—and no bathroom—and we always ask the Lord what we can do to help.

An Incredible Journey

In the 2009 inaugural edition of Joy Junction's *Good News Gazette*, we mentioned a desire to run a lunch wagon that would be filled with coffee, soup, sandwiches, and other food with which we could bless the homeless. The plan was for the wagon to visit areas frequented by the homeless and provide a lifeline in the form of food, drink, and prayer. This lifeline of hope would let those using its services know that someone cares. And it might even save a life—or more.

As mentioned earlier, a few days later, I received an e-mail from a very dear friend of Joy Junction, a local businessman from Summit Electric Supply. He said he had gone online and found something on eBay that may work for us. I took a look and was immediately excited. The vehicle looked like it was everything we needed to make our vision a reality.

The problem was that the vehicle was in Florida's West Palm Beach. I thought and prayed and sensed that the Lord wanted me to personally go and pick it up. I mentioned this to the donor, who immediately responded that if I was sure I wanted to do this, he would pay for my air ticket. What a wonderful blessing!

A few days later, along with a former employee from Joy Junction's corporate office who offered to come along with me, we set off. Those three days were truly a whirlwind of activity but also provided an opportunity for me to reflect on the Lord's goodness—both to me personally and to Joy Junction.

Day 1: The Journey Begins

Sleep eluded me for much of the night as I lay there tossing and turning, waiting for the alarm to go at 4:45 a.m. to signal the time to get up and catch the 7:10 plane for Florida.

I stumbled out of bed, took two aspirin to ward off the painful rumblings of an approaching headache, forsook my usual chai latte, and turned on the shower.

After a much quicker than usual trip to the airport down a relatively deserted road, I arrived at a packed airline ticket counter, where I met Rich.

There was a quick trip through security and then time for a quick stop for chai (and a piece of ham and green chili quiche). The lady serving me the chai looked at me and said, "Oh, I didn't think you'd have time to travel."

A little taken aback, I answered, "I'm on the way to pick up a donation for Joy Junction—a lunch wagon."

"Oh," she said. That was it, other than a comment that my quiche would be at the microwave. Oh, the joys of being known!

We made our way to the line for the plane. The adventure was beginning. Our plan was to get to West Palm Beach to pick up the lunch wagon and drive it the five or six hours north to Tallahassee before we stopped for the night.

Boarding the plane, I told a cheery Southwest flight attendant I was hoping for lots of jokes.

"Maybe singing," he said with a smile.

A few minutes later, we were airborne for the first leg of our journey, which would take us through Houston and Tampa on our way to West Palm Beach.

The flight was smooth and uneventful, but toward the end I was thinking the flight attendant had let me down on his promise to sing. Just then, he burst into song, singing something like, "We love you, you love us, and we're much faster than a bus. Marry one of us, and you'll fly free."

I love Southwest Airlines humor! It continued just prior to the next leg of the flight, with one of the crew members asking people to hurry up and get all the formalities disposed of so we could take off. He said his wife had just called, and his mother-in-law was getting through security. He wanted the plane in the air before she made it, he said. Most of the passengers laughed.

The Houston–Tampa leg of our trip was pretty smooth, and I passed the time by reading a captivating, eye-opening, and horrifying book by Nick Reding titled *Methland: The Death and Life of an American Small Town*.

After a quick layover in Tampa and time to take care of some e-mails and phone calls, we boarded another plane for West Palm Beach. Making my way up the aisle, I couldn't help but overhear hear one side of a conversation. Speaking on his cell phone rather loudly, a man was saying, "I'm fifty-two, I don't do drugs, and I don't want kids."

Hmm, I thought. *Now we've got that taken care of, tell me how you really feel.* I wondered about the other half of that conversation.

The flight from Tampa to West Palm Beach was short and uneventful, and about forty-five minutes or so later, we touched down. The humidity hung in the air, even in the air-conditioned airport. While I love mountains and the ocean, humidity is definitely not for me.

Walking outside the airport, where a dealership employee was waiting to give us a ride to the truck, we were assaulted by even worse humidity. We arrived at the dealership a few minutes later and saw the beautiful lunch wagon. We were introduced to the general manager, a man not shy about sharing his faith, who asked us about Joy Junction and how I began the shelter over two decades before. When I shared with him what the lunch truck would be used for, he seemed delighted. I think he initially believed we would be selling food as a profit-making enterprise. His mouth dropped when I told him what we had in mind.

After signing all the papers necessary to transfer ownership of the lunch truck to Joy Junction, we were on our way. We prayed, asking for the Lord's blessing, and Rich started driving what the dealership staff called our "lunch mobile 747."

As we drove, we tuned in to a variety of country music stations (each fading out of range quickly) to make sure we stayed alert and awake. In a couple of hours we pulled into a rest stop area for some food. Rich had a wrap, and I somehow ended up with another piece of ham quiche—but minus the green chili. This wasn't New Mexico.

We had another couple of hours before reaching Tallahassee. Rich continued driving, for which I was grateful. This gave me the opportunity to write as we moved down the road. Even while sitting in the 747 and rolling toward our hotel, ideas were beginning to swirl in my mind about how we could best bless the homeless with our new acquisition. We already had a staff member who was very interested in being involved in the lunch truck operation. I was pumped about this new ministry!

We continued driving, and I kept on answering e-mails and writing. I also checked on some of the early Albuquerque municipal election results by going to Facebook. My life without Facebook and BlackBerry? Did I even have one?

Within about fifty miles of our hotel I was just worn out. I felt grimy, my legs were aching, my back hurt, and I just wanted rest. How grateful I was for a motel room, a clean bed, and a place to stay. My thoughts went to why we were doing this cross-country jaunt in the first place: to make living easier for the homeless and perhaps even save people's lives by giving them food and water.

How thankful I was for this wonderful donor who had purchased the vehicle for our use, and for the Lord who continues sustaining this amazing ministry.

A few minutes after we pulled into our motel and checked in, I thanked the Lord for his goodness and collapsed into bed!

Day 2: The Incredible Journey Continues

It was 9:30 a.m. in Florida—7:30 back home—and time to get on the road. Our marathon trek in the 747 lunch wagon continued on to Dallas.

Note to the TSA folks: if you unscrew liquids in my suitcase, would you please screw the cap back on so they don't spill all over my suitcase? Thanks!

As I stepped out of the hotel, it was so humid that my glasses fogged up. This was just so not me. I couldn't wait for Albuquerque!

A chai and a sausage piadini would have to suffice for now. I made my way back to the lunch wagon through the parking lot. It would be next to impossible to miss this beautiful vehicle, so I didn't have to wander directionally challenged around the parking lot in search of my little Pontiac Vibe.

After asking the Lord's blessing on the day and our travel, we took off, Rich behind the wheel and me beside him, e-mailing and taking care of JJ business from the BlackBerry—my mobile office! As I did so, I was listening to the words of the song "Live Like You're Dying." This country tune had an obvious biblical theme. How would we change the way we live if we knew we only had a short time left? I can speak only for myself, but I think there might be some significant changes.

We had an uneventful morning and pulled into a Chick-fil-A for a quick lunch before making our way over to Jackson, Mississippi, where we stopped to feed the 747. After we pulled into a gas station with heavily barred windows, my attempts to pay at the pump were met with a computer-generated message telling me to see the attendant. I did just that, but when I offered him a credit card, he said somewhat tersely, "We don't take no credit cards." We didn't stop to inquire further. We just thanked him and went a few hundred feet across the street to a station that did.

Our next stop was for coffee and a couple of other small purchases. I used my Visa debit card and was very surprised when it was denied. A call a few minutes later to my credit union revealed that the credit function of the debit card had been uniformly disabled for all members in about six states due to data that had been compromised somewhere and somehow earlier that year. Fortunately, I had an alternative method of payment. While I later learned the debit function still worked, it took a call to the credit union to find that out. Another on-the-road adventure.

We plowed on, driving I-20 west to Dallas, so somewhere west of Shreveport and about 170 miles east of Dallas, we stopped for a fast-food supper. We didn't want to stray too far off the highway, and as a friend told me, "Fine dining off the highway is an oxymoron!" My buffalo wings with honey mustard sauce, a small order of fries, and a tiny cup of coffee testified to how true that was. A few minutes later, we were on our way. *Dallas, here we come!* What a whirlwind trip this was. As usual, my BlackBerry kept me in touch with everything and everyone.

Close to our hotel and very tired, Rich and I were encouraged to see the Soulman's Barbeque Restaurant with a Jesus is Lord sign.

A few minutes later, with the help of the GPS on the BlackBerry, we pulled into our hotel. The good Lord had given us another day to serve him before collapsing into bed.

Day 3: The Incredible Journey Concludes

The third day of a road trip needs to begin with two things: prayer and a visit Starbucks. While talking to the barista, I said I was on the way home to Albuquerque. Another employee overheard me and said she loved Hatch green chili. She'd never been to New Mexico, but friends regularly sent her chili from there. I left with my chai, happy to have reminded her of New Mexico. Maybe I made her day a bit better.

Rich and I sharing the driving, and I e-mailed prolifically when not behind the wheel. Running Joy Junction is a never-ending job, even in the cab of a 747 lunch wagon, and it is definitely never boring.

Later in the afternoon we arrived at Amarillo. It would be hard not to pay a visit to the Big Texan, home of the free seventy-two-ounce steak—free, that is, if you are able to devour the gargantuan slice of meat and sides in an hour or less. I'd been there a number of times, but Rich had never visited. He had a much-smaller-than-seventy-two-ounce steak, and I tried a heart-stopping, artery-clogging chicken fried steak. Both the food and the service were excellent.

Bone-chilling temperatures assaulted us when we left the restaurant, which made me thank the Lord for the safety of a warm truck and the promise of a warm and safe house and a comfortable bed when the trip was finished. I was unaware of the homeless situation in Amarillo, but I breathed a quick prayer for the Lord's blessing and protection for those homeless souls who, for whatever reason, would have no place to stay that night.

We fed the 747 and started off on the last leg of our long and tiring journey. We were in New Mexico only a short while later. And we were there with a food truck—a very tangible lifeline for the homeless. It was so good to be home again and enjoy the beautiful sunset as we got closer to Albuquerque. I so much appreciate New Mexico, where I have spent more than half of my life.

Hope and Help for the Hungry in Downtown Albuquerque and Beyond

A largely deserted lot in downtown Albuquerque that backs onto railroad tracks took on new life and hope for a while last Sunday. It was there that about fifty homeless people enjoyed a sack lunch, a beverage, and the offer of a blanket from Joy Junction.

Providing a Sunday meal downtown was a new venture for us. While we serve more than ten thousand meals each month at our 4500 Second Street Southwest location, we had never before served meals off-site. But when I learned that there was a lack of resources downtown on Sunday for the city's growing homeless population, it seemed a natural thing to do.

After all, I figured, it's rather ironic that the Lord's Day was a day of lack for the city's poor and homeless rather than a time of bounty and provision.

Wanting to make sure we did everything right, we checked on the appropriate city requirements and talked to the owner of the lot at First and Iron, asking whether he would be willing to allow us to hold the event there. He graciously agreed.

We started preparing. Our kitchen manager at Joy Junction and his crew put together some great sack lunches. Then, Sunday at one o'clock, our crew headed over, taking 150 lunches. Although I wasn't really sure about the size of the need and how many people would turn up, within a few minutes of setting up shop a line of people had formed. They were all hungry, extremely well behaved, and very grateful.

We served about one hundred meals to our fifty or so guests. A number of people asked if they could take another sack lunch to feed a hungry friend; others asked for themselves, for assurance they would have something to eat that evening. How tragic that any of us have to wonder where our next meal is coming from.

Many of those we served were understandably reticent to share the circumstances that had led to their plight. Yet one man told local media he had been traveling the country looking for work but had run out of money and gas. Besides that, his unemployment check hadn't arrived. But at least he now had a full belly, something for which he was very grateful.

Joy Junction outreach coordinator Kathy Sotelo said the outreach touched her deeply. "Taking part in such a wonderful event was so heartwarming. Knowing that we made a difference of that kind is unlike anything else I've ever experienced." As Kathy saw the weary and sometimes emotionally and physically weighed down people take a sack lunch, she was grateful to have had a moment to chat with them. She said, "Hearing some of their stories made me feel so much more connected."

The Joy Junction volunteer coordinator was equally impacted. For him, "Probably the most moving sight was the line of homeless individuals sitting on the curb, devouring their lunch, drinking their coffee or juice, and carefully protecting their newly received blankets. They had their own little personal space, staying in their comfort zones, making sure not to waste any crumb of food or drop of liquid."

Our staff member began thinking about the solidarity shared by our lunchtime friends. He said that although there was a variety of people and backgrounds represented there, something special happened. "While they began their meals as loners," the staff member said, "they opened up and started to share stories. They began introducing themselves to each other and exchanging stories of their individual migratory habits. They talked about where to go for food, who was not being nice to the homeless in downtown, and invariably they commented about Joy Junction always trying to help."

With the Lord's continued help, we will keep serving Albuquerque's hungry—at Joy Junction, downtown, and beyond. Summit Electric Supply's generous donation of the Lifeline of Hope has helped us dramatically expand that initial outreach. The Lifeline can, quite literally, make the difference between life and death to someone hungry, dehydrated, cold, and frightened.

We launched our mission with the 747 lunch wagon on Sunday, November 8, 2009, at one o'clock at the corner of First and Iron, and then we made our way to a number of other locations. It was stocked to serve about 150 people on its launch, and now we typically feed as many as 300 meals on an average Sunday at various homeless "hot spots" throughout the city, along with hundreds more during the other days of the week we serve.

I am very excited about this new outreach, something so needed in this difficult economy, but I am counting on my readers to provide financial and volunteer support. That will allow us to keep on keepin' on in our constant effort to minister to the needs of the hungry and homeless in Albuquerque. Will you help us?

Made Whole by Jesus

Lynn: Diligent and Faithful

While Lynn is alcohol-free today, that hasn't always been the case. I sat down with Lynn and asked what caused her to start abusing alcohol. She said it was in part due to wanting to be accepted by her friends. But it was also because of a difficult childhood, which she said wasn't good to begin with. When her biological father abandoned them, she was left with her half sister and adopted mother.

"I was the constant reminder to my mother of the infidelity that took place in her marriage that led to the divorce. And I was the sad reminder to my sister of why daddy was no longer with us. I was always mindful of how misplaced I was, and how much my mom regretted keeping me." Lynn said living in an affluent neighborhood didn't help, either. "My sister and I were the kids no one else could play with, since we were the only ones in the neighborhood who didn't have a dad around. My sister blamed me for her friends no longer coming around, and she blamed mom for why her friends looked the other way." That's why she got involved with the "outcasts" in the neighborhood, and the drinking started.

To fit in, to be cool, and to cope, Lynn's drinking continued in the military. When she got out of the service she entered a bad marriage and continued her drinking. She drank so much that she was unable to fulfill her obligations to her children. "I was shunning all of my responsibilities. I thought that escaping was the best thing to do. I drank more to deal with problems I was creating for myself. The more

I drank to escape my problems, the more problems I created for myself and my family."

Lynn was what is referred to as a "functioning alcoholic." That means she didn't pass out drunk. She got jobs bartending, not exactly the best employment for an alcoholic. Even while she worked, she said, "I would be drunker than some people I was cutting off serving. But I never really passed out. I just got to the point where I would get drunk enough to either get really violent or just lash out at people because of the pain I was feeling."

Lynn said she also gained weight and had a lot of self-esteem issues, which caused her to push people away. "I'd rather be drunk and alone than put myself in a position to be hurt again."

She described her husband as a drinker, into drugs, and rarely around. "I guess I did marry my father after all. My mother of course blamed me for my marriage being bad, and questioned me about why I had children with this man. She always brought up my childhood, and when she did she would never forget to say, 'You're stupid.' (I graduated high school with a 3.75 GPA.) She would always say, 'You're lazy and worthless,' and 'You're fat.' (Mom isn't exactly skinny.) She constantly called me a terrible mother (like mother, like daughter). She threatened to have my kids taken away if I didn't shape up."

All of this helped the bottle become Lynn's comfort, as opposed to her husband and children. She said, "I broke my word to my children and made promises I couldn't keep, and I knew at the time I wouldn't keep them."

Because she could hold a job and pay her bills, the idea of being an alcoholic never really occurred to Lynn. After all, she thought, it wasn't like she was drunk and sleeping under a bridge. She added, "I thought I was better off than alcoholics were. But they could see the consequences of their choices, and I couldn't."

I asked Lynn if she had any influences in her life telling her that maybe she was drinking too much. At that time, she didn't. She wasn't raised in what she would describe as a religious household, even though her grandfather was a minister. She said, "I had to develop a relationship with God on my own, which now I see was a blessing. However, I turned from God, believing there must be no God, since, if there was a God, why is my life so terrible? I separated myself from God and had to find my way back to him."

Lynn said her second husband helped her do that by giving her a better life and hope. And he helped her stop drinking. While she was better, she was not fully healed, but that was to change. "A little over five years ago, I gave my life and everything to the Lord," Lynn said. "He took away the drinking and the urges." I asked her if there were any precipitating circumstances that caused her to give her life to Jesus. She said it was drinking and realizing that God had a better way for her to live. She said, "This wasn't the life God had planned for me. He had a better one, with no stress and with not abusing my body or myself the way that I was. God had been with me the whole time. I just never acknowledged it."

When Lynn came to Albuquerque, she said she began losing her faith and wanted to start drinking again. "I couldn't see it as a test of faith. I just saw signs of losing faith and letting the actions of others guide me. I forgot the life God wanted for me, that he had taken those feelings away and that I needed to get back on the right track. I left the job and went back to Iowa to help my mom, who had cancer."

After Lynn's mother got better, she and her husband decided to return to Albuquerque. They felt they needed to strengthen their relationship with the Lord, so they joined our faith-based life recovery program. "It made me look at my life closer and brought out some issues that I hadn't seen before. It brought me closer to God as well. It makes you realize God's will for us and the way he wants us to live and treat each other. He wants for us to have a happy life, not an addicted life."

Where would Lynn and her husband (as well as many others) be without the services offered by Joy Junction? Her answer is that they would either be living in a tent or under a bridge—or in jail. She added, "In extreme cases, I could have been dead from alcohol poisoning. I know in Iowa there is no shelter like this available in the whole state. They have only one place to go, and they split up the family. Also, it's not faith based. It's just a recovery program."

I asked Lynn what she would say to the thousands of donors who make Joy Junction (which receives no government funding) an ongoing reality. She said, "I would say just continue giving, because without their blessings, we aren't blessed. I'm from Iowa, so I'll use an example of planting corn. You plant a seed, just a little seed, and with that seed a corn plant grows. On that plant there are ears of corn and with those ears of corn a whole family can be fed. That is how it works with giving. It multiplies. With just one tiny donation, a lot of people can benefit. Everything they donate is just a true blessing for us here."

I asked Lynn if she had one wish, what it would be? She said to continue on the road she and her husband are on currently. "Hopefully, we can get out and get our own place and be able to share the love that we've experienced and tell our story to others."

Joy Junction resident services manager Joel Steen described Lynn in two words: diligent and faithful. Those are some pretty good and accurate words.

Donna: No Longer an Addict

For Donna, coming to Albuquerque and Joy Junction was a return to God's will, her recovery, and a new spirituality. Donna left a sober house in Connecticut and came to Albuquerque by bus. She had enough money to stay in a hotel for two days. When that ran out, she called a domestic violence hotline (she was a domestic violence victim in Connecticut) and they recommended she call Joy Junction.

Donna was at Joy Junction initially for three weeks, and then she left for three weeks, which she called a major mistake. She returned to continue Joy Junction's life recovery program.

Donna told me things are now going quite well for her. "I think finally, after close to two and a half years, I have actually reached my second step (of a twelve-step program). I actually feel like coming here was kind of a blessing, and this is where I was meant to be."

Many people don't really know what it's like to battle an addiction, to crave a drink or a drug. Donna says it becomes the most important thing on your mind. "You put it before anybody and anything else, because you don't want to deal with what's going on. You don't want to deal with what you're feeling. You just get used to the idea that it's easier to go through life, you know, numb."

That is what makes one an addict in the first place. The substance you crave masks the pain of addressing issues you should be dealing with, but can't. Donna agrees. "You convince yourself you're dealing with them as you go out and drink and drug about them, but you're not. You don't feel any of it."

I asked Donna if she had ever slept outside in Albuquerque. She said she had slept outside another local mission when she voluntarily left Joy Junction. "I left with people who had substance abuse issues, and before I came back I spent a night out in front of that mission. That was not fun. The experience was really scary. Sleeping on the sidewalk there, and the drug dealer coming by. He scared me and woke me up, telling me to shut up. Finally he swore at me and the line of twelve other people who didn't have any other place to go."

After that, Donna returned to the safety of Joy Junction. I asked her how staying with us has helped her. She said, "I think I've come farther in my recovery with my addiction and personally than I have in the almost three years that I've gotten sober—two years and nine months since I stopped drinking or drugging."

Donna said having a relationship with God has helped her. Looking back, she realizes that God had given her signs about her life. When she did things her way, when she didn't listen to God, she abused alcohol and drugs, and things became bad pretty quickly. But when she did things God's way, her life turned around. So much so, Donna said, that God has taken away the compulsion for her to drink.

She praised Joy Junction's life recovery curriculum, the Christ in Power Program. "It's really wonderful, especially for people in addiction, and even for people no longer in addiction but who need to continue focusing on the Lord." Even though she is no longer in addiction, Donna says she still asks the Lord daily for help not to drink.

I asked her what would be her one wish if she had one. Her response was "That Joy Junction continue to operate with what you've got planned for the future here and all that I've heard about."

Since people give to missions like Joy Junction and sometimes wonder where their donation is going, Donna said, "The money given to Joy Junction gets stretched as far as it can, and unfortunately it's not enough. There are needs that aren't able to be met here. There are things that require money to be fixed. The program is a wonderful program, but unfortunately money and finances are an issue."

Joel Steen, Joy Junction resident services manager, said, "Donna has interacted often in class and has not shied away from telling the truth about her past, even though it may show her defects. She has stayed faithful to the program and has not only reached out to others with help, but has accepted help as well."

Nancy: "It Feels Good to Laugh Again"

Nancy never expected to be at Joy Junction, but who does? Troubles for Nancy, fifty-four, and her son Jeff, twenty-seven, began in Arkansas when she couldn't pay the rent. She had no job, no money, and no reserve funds available to tap into. She and Jeff were brought to New Mexico by her daughter's ex-father-in-law.

She said, "We were living with another family member, and they got evicted because only one of them had been paying the bills. The other one was on drugs. We heard about Joy Junction from a family friend. That was nineteen months ago."

Nancy said Joy Junction has done so much for her. "It has kept us off the street and has kept me from going back to a life of drugs and alcohol. I had a past history of drug and alcohol abuse." She credited CIPP. Nancy says, "The nine-month program has helped me be a stronger person and renewed my faith. It's brought me closer to God by going through the classes and being able to pray more. I wasn't praying as much as I am now. It has helped me be a whole lot more appreciative of the things I have, as well as being thankful for people trying to help me. Now I want to help others who are in the same situation as me."

Not surprisingly, staying alcohol- and drug-free has helped Nancy improve her relationship with her son. "The program has helped us get closer together mentally, and it has made me see the error of my ways when raising my son. Jeff doesn't hate me anymore. It has also helped him with spiritual guidance, and he's come out of his shell and made friends ... He and I talk to each other more, help each other more, and are there for each other. It has made me a better parent. He had a lot of questions about faith, and talking with Chaplain Gene, he's found some answers. He found a place in this world where he can talk to people, and he is now willing to talk to and help others as well. He smiles a lot more these days."

Jeff contributed this insight: "Joy Junction has helped me with my anger and my depression issues. Being in the life recovery classes helped me come out of the shell I was in. It also gave me the confidence to do things by myself. Before I got here I wouldn't talk to anyone." He added, "I appreciate Joy Junction allowing us to be in the life recovery program to make the changes I needed in mine and my mom's life."

Nancy recalled talking to a former staff member, whom she described as being "very sweet and helpful when I called for us to come in. Every one of the staff members here is a godsend. I want to thank Dr. Reynalds personally for having a place where people can go who need to talk to someone, who have been abused in every way. We need more places like Joy Junction in this world. It has helped me come to terms with the things in my life that I didn't want to face for over thirty-five years without breaking down and crying. Now I'm not such an angry, bitter, and hateful person."

Diana Lane, a driver at Joy Junction, said she has noticed significant changes in both Nancy and Jeff. "Nancy has become more friendly and helpful. She's starting to enjoy her life. The changes in Jeff are even more significant," Diana said. "He has more incentive now and never says he can't or won't. Now he says he can and will."

Nancy concluded that while she needs more spiritual guidance, "I haven't felt this good in forty-five years. It feels good to laugh again."

Brad: A Bus Ticket Back

Homeless people roam the ninety-five-degree streets of Las Vegas, some going through trash cans, some sitting there with signs asking for money, and some just sitting. No one seems to pay a whole lot of attention to them. They might almost be part of the scenery. During a recent trip to Las Vegas with friends, I found Brad on Fremont Street.

According to *Wikipedia*, "Fremont Street is ... the second most famous street in the Las Vegas Valley after the Las Vegas Strip. [It was] named in honor of explorer John Charles Frémont and [is] located in the heart of the downtown casino corridor." With all the bustling activity, liquor, vendors, and casinos, experiencing Fremont Street was something akin to spending a concert night at the Hard Rock Pavilion, the State Fair, and all our casinos rolled into one. It's known as the "Fremont Street experience." Brad is a part of the "experience" that is not talked about so much.

I asked Brad, who was in a wheelchair, if he was hungry. He said he was, so I gave him a gift card for a fast-food restaurant. He agreed to talk with me for a few minutes about being homeless in Las Vegas. He said he is surviving, but life is difficult. Brad said he had been in Las Vegas for eighteen months and homeless for about five years total and came there because he believed he could find work. He's been in a wheelchair for about six months.

Being homeless in Las Vegas "sucks," he said. "Pardon my English, but it sucks. I shattered my ankle, lost my job, and of course I ended up losing my apartment 'cause I couldn't pay for it. That's what happens when you work under the table; you don't get no benefits."

Brad described a typical day on the streets of Las Vegas. "Panhandling to survive, to eat, to have a drink so you can go to sleep on the bare ground. I have a lot of health problems all of a sudden, and I won't take pills, so I ended up drinking, ended up getting addicted to that. I should have took the darn pills," he said, laughing. Brad said he has been attacked and robbed three times—close to where I was talking to him.

He said, "I was trying to find a place to sleep because I try to stay away from all the others, because they're the ones that steal from you. They're the ones that attack you. You have no friends out here. You just have people that want to take from you."

Brad said he gets moved on a lot by the police. "It's constant. It depends on their moods and which officer, but yeah, they make me move." I asked Brad if there was a law against panhandling. "Yeah, but there's not supposed to be a law against flying a sign that doesn't ask for money, but they gave me a ticket for it. Oh, they're gonna give me probably five days in jail."

I asked Brad what he would say to those who claim he could get help if he really wanted to. In a curious twist of reasoning, his response was that drinking makes some area homeless services inaccessible to him. The alcohol he uses to numb the pain has now resulted in his waking up with the shakes. "So I have to have a drink to calm down and cure my stomach, and I can't use the services," he said.

As our conversation continued, I learned that Brad had worked all his life. He said he has been a carpenter, an electrician, a painter, and a gardener. He said he's fighting for disability benefits.

If he had one wish, what would it be? He said it would be to get a bus ticket back to Santa Cruz, California. While he doesn't have family there, Brad said he does have friends, access to health care, and a place he can get a job. Tears ran down his cheeks as he talked.

I asked Brad if I could pray with him, and he gladly accepted. Will you also say a prayer for Brad?

April: "People Have Rights"

A trip to Las Vegas is one people talk about for years. For the city's homeless and hungry, however, the experience is one most would prefer to forget.

While spending a few days in Las Vegas, I encountered April and her three children on Fremont Street. After giving them a gift card for a fast-food restaurant, I asked her if she would mind talking to me a bit about her experience of homelessness.

April told me how she and her family ended up on Fremont Street. She said she paid her landlord's wife seven hundred dollars on the second of the month—one hundred dollars in cash, and a money order for six hundred dollars. But she was unaware that at about the same time she was paying her rent her landlord was at the local courthouse, starting the eviction process. As a result, April said, "The marshal came in and kicked me and my three kids out."

April continued, "My kids are bipolar. My son hasn't taken his medication in over a week. The landlord won't let me back in the house to get their food, their clothing, nothing. The pound came and took all our animals, and I have to pay to get them out. I have no money."

April said the police haven't harassed her. She said, "They come by and check on me, and ask me if I have plenty of water. They make sure that my kids are okay."

At the time we talked, April and her family had been homeless for about two weeks. I asked her how she was handling the experience. April said it had been rough. "Right now I'm staying in my Suburban in a friend's backyard, and it's been really hot. It's been really hard for me and my kids. I told myself I'd never do it again, and this is what happens. I end up being back on the street again with my kids."

April gets food stamps and social security, but her family's need is greater than the assistance she receives. April said she's a Christian but had been unable to get any help from area churches.

I asked her how the kids were coping with the situation. She said they handle it, one day at a time, but her son gets pretty upset. I told April that her children had beautiful smiles and that they must help her keep going. She said, "My kids do keep me going every day. If it wasn't for my kids I'd be in the nut ward."

I asked April what she would like people to know about her family's homelessness. She said she wants them to realize that landlords should not be able to bully people. "People need to stick up for what they have. They have rights. The owner of the property is supposed to make sure the house has air, heat, everything. And that's what the landlord is supposed to do. He is not to bully people. If landlords don't live up to their responsibilities, then how are you supposed to survive?"

I asked April how she feels when she wakes up every morning. She said, "I want to cry." I asked one of the kids how they feel, and the youngster replied, "I feel sad because I don't have a home, and I feel bad for other people."

April said if she had one wish, it would be for a house.

I added, "And some food maybe?"

April said, "Yes, for my kids. I could go without for quite a while. I don't care about me. I just want my kids to have the food."

April said she's out on the streets every day, "because it gets so hot where we're at, so I have to come down here to sit where it's nice and cool. And then I have to walk back to where I'm at."

As April told me her mom and dad used to say, "You gotta take it one day at a time. If you don't, the Devil is going to bring you down."

That's so true. How else can you stand hours, days, and weeks of wondering where your next meal and night's shelter are coming from?

Tom: A Deep Homeless Quagmire

Amidst the hustle and bustle of Fremont Street, I found Tom. Tom has been homeless for five or six months, and he attributes his difficulty in getting a job to his age (being close to sixty years old), a larceny conviction resulting in spending some time locked up, and a difficult economy in Las Vegas. "If you don't have a job, it's kind of hard to get one," Tom said.

Tom said government benefits paid his rent for about three months, but then the assistance ran out. He said he had looked for jobs at several small restaurants but didn't land anything. "They already have a full shift or whatever. They just won't hire me."

I asked Tom where he slept at night. He said, "Sometimes I don't sleep anywhere, but at times I find a little hole and go to sleep." He wasn't sure where he would sleep that coming night.

I was curious what Tom would say about living on the streets of what is arguably America's most well-known city. "I try to hustle to eat, and hope I get enough to get a motel room or whatever." As for shelters, Tom has stayed in some in the past, but no more. "I had a crime that happened twenty years or so ago, and they looked me up on the computer. Then all of a sudden they told me I can't stay there, and I'm not allowed on their property."

I asked Tom what he would like people to know about him and his experiences of being homeless in Las Vegas. He said, "It would be a blessing if they could pitch in and help in some kind of way." Tom responded quickly when I asked him if he had one wish what it would be. He said, "Somewhere to sleep tonight and something good to eat."

I was troubled as I left Tom. I'd given him a fast-food gift card, and I chatted and prayed with him. But I didn't really know him or the troubles he had faced that resulted in him panhandling on a late Saturday afternoon on Fremont Street. What were his dreams and fears? Where were his parents? Had he ever been married? Did he have children? Spending only a few minutes with Tom, I felt I had no right asking him these sorts of questions. But I wondered how long Tom—or any other homeless and hungry person in Las Vegas—would last before sinking down into an even deeper homeless quagmire.

It's easy to provide all the clichéd answers and assume, "Well, if that were me …" Well, it's not you, and it's not me. It's Tom. Before you judge him, walk a mile in his shoes, and say a prayer for him as well!

Edward: You're Never Too Old to Kick an Addiction

It's never easy being homeless, and the difficulties are compounded when you're seventy-five years old. That's the plight faced by Edward, one of our Joy Junction guests and a participant in our life recovery program. Edward is a retired electrician who lives on a small amount of social security money. It is definitely not enough money to make ends meet, especially when battling an alcohol addiction.

Edward was evicted from his apartment because his money went to alcohol instead of paying his rent. "They brought me a notice from their lawyer saying that I had been unruly and arguing with other tenants. I decided not to even worry about it. If they didn't want me in the building, I didn't want to be there, either. That was my attitude."

Edward admitted he had probably been unruly as a result of being intoxicated. Still, he was angry about being homeless—and scared. "I have slept outside a few times, but I certainly do not like it out on the streets. It's dangerous."

Edward knew he needed more than just shelter. He had to find a program to help him with his addiction. He was aware of Joy Junction, so a few months ago he began as an overnight guest and was accepted when he applied to join our life recovery program. He said things are usually good for him these days and that he enjoys being around people who are recovering from addiction issues. "I have made friends, and I know some who have done well and actually overcome their addiction. No one can tell what tomorrow will bring us, but I do get hope from that and from the friends I've made here at Joy Junction. I think if they can do that, I can do that too."

In addition to his addiction, Edward also has some health problems. He broke his hip and a shoulder and doesn't really know where he would be without Joy Junction. He said, "I knew of Joy Junction. I had heard of it from my work with the Salvation Army." He added, "I also worked at a mission a long time ago helping others. I like helping other people, but now I'm the one who needs it. I ask for help every night from the Lord, and I get answers."

Being at Joy Junction has helped him in his fight against alcoholism, but his battle is never easy. "The help I need is in the area of defeating an addiction. You never really defeat it, but overcoming my addiction and being able to get around on my scooter is also helpful too. I like being here because I feel strength and faith, and I hope that eventually I can leave Joy Junction--but not right at this time."

I asked Edward what he would like to tell the thousands of wonderful donors who give to Joy Junction each month. Without them, I told him, we couldn't be there for him. Edward made it clear he appreciates our donors. He said, "They made it possible for me to have hope and resume faith. I've been a Christian for a while, a long while, but I strayed away. Their donations make this all possible. There is no way I could be here unless Joy Junction was helped by other people." He added, "I like our life recovery classes. I like being around the other people who are recovering and who have faith in God and Jesus."

I asked Edward if he had one wish what it would be. He said, "I'd pray for strength that I won't give up, and I don't plan on giving up. I get strength from the other people here, the teachers, and the staff. It makes me very hopeful that there are things to come."

Please pray for Edward. Joy Junction resident services manager Joel Steen says Edward has been a faithful life recovery program participant. Joel said, "Edward attends classes regularly and is always at his station when it is his turn to volunteer. What I enjoy about him the most is his smile. I have never seen him without it. He is also honest about his recovery needs and participates in classes."

You'd Be Surprised Who Hates the Homeless

Johnny: "We Are Vapors"

It's hard enough being homeless. When you're robbed of the possessions you have and the few dollars you might get for a day's labor, that just adds insult to injury. Sadly, that happens all the time. When our staff first heard about these incidents, we assumed that it was random street violence. But then we heard these attacks were apparently being carried out by non homeless individuals driving, in some cases, reasonably nice vehicles.

With that in mind, I asked Lisa Woodward, Joy Junction transportation manager, to investigate. Lisa has an ear to the ground about what occurs on the streets. To investigate, Lisa began what she dubbed a weeklong information scavenger hunt.

Lisa said, "I have lived among and worked with the homeless population for almost eight years and have seen us being treated with disdain, disrespect, and cruelty. However, I never saw that we would be targets in what boils down to a hate crime."

Lisa explained what she meant. When she started digging into these crimes, which apparently happen quite frequently on the streets of downtown Albuquerque, every victim she spoke with said the perpetrator made some comment like "You're homeless anyway. It's not like you have to pay rent with this money." Lisa said, "This made my heart skip, and I walked back to the van, feeling rage I hadn't felt in years."

Lisa was drawn to Johnny, who has lived on the streets for close to thirty years. She is unsure of his exact age, but she would guess him to be in his late eighties. "He is a gentle and calm spirit who cannot function in mainstream society. He asks for little, and to those who live around him, he gives all."

Lisa made her way into the alley where Johnny has his pop-up house and tapped on the side. Johnny appeared and invited her in. To her surprise, he was eating a hamburger, a meal he was appearing to relish. Lisa said, "He caught my glance and smiled back, explaining that sometimes the restaurant nearby would let him sweep the parking lot for a meal. I asked him if I could ask a few questions while he ate. He said, 'Of course, Miss Lisa. Why is your heart heavy tonight, child?'"

She asked Johnny if he had heard of these crimes that seemed to be multiplying, or if he thought they were something new. She also asked him if he had ever been attacked. He said he had heard of them but that he had not been a victim. He told Lisa he was "the wrong homeless class to be rolled by them."

Lisa said, "My head cocked, and I said, 'Johnny, homeless is homeless.' He said, 'No, child. Homeless is not homeless.'"

Lisa gave Johnny a cigarette and waited for him to continue. He told Lisa there are three "classes" of homeless people. "There are the homeless that you and Joy Junction primarily serve," Johnny said. "They have fallen on hard times, have abuse problems, or are 'system homeless.' Their parents never really stood on solid ground nor their parents before them, so they were never given the skills to keep a job, pay rent, car payments and do all the other things necessary for life."

Johnny said there are also what he called "warrior" homeless. "They're in small-time drug sales, drink a lot, and are in and out of jail. Some are gang members. They want to stay under law enforcement radar."

Then there are "street homeless." Johnny said, "That is me, Miss Lisa. Now don't get me wrong. I have been known to have whisky to help keep this old body warm and will say here and now I will use it again, but only when available."

He smiled and continued. "Lisa, my people don't come out in the day, and at night we are vapors, the shadow you thought you might have seen. I don't panhandle, and I don't steal. I sweep here for food and there for smokes. I receive social security and a little from the veterans. It pays for my medication and propane for my stove. I walk to Tingley Beach and fish when I get hungry for my mama's fish and chips. My class of homeless does not exist."

Johnny told Lisa that people who are just getting by hate the homeless served by Joy Junction. He said, "These rolls are hate crimes. The people who function every day through a shelter are tagged by those who just hocked their car title to pay the rent or buy food. They know your homeless will be fed and pay nothing to sleep warm and take a hot shower. Miss Lisa, they feel your homeless people have more, and it is all given to them."

For Lisa, the sky began brightening as she looked at Johnny with tears in her eyes. "I told him he did exist and that he was a very special soul. I handed him the rest of my pack of cigarettes and hugged him, promising I would see him soon."

As the sun came up, Lisa drove back to Joy Junction, her mind teeming with what she had heard. She said, "The misconceptions about the homeless have always bothered me, but I had not felt anger like this since I encountered a man at a convenience store who recognized me from Joy Junction and asked how I could sleep with a bunch of dirty bums." Lisa added, "I implore those who see us downtown or anywhere, flying a sign or sitting on the corner waiting for the day to go by, come to Joy Junction and take a tour before you judge us. See what our reality is. The lights will come on at six o'clock in the morning, and there is *no* snooze button to hit for just fifteen more minutes. There is no stretching and wandering to the kitchen for a cup of coffee in your robe. With their daily struggles, many see no hope. Suffering a vicious attack can be the final indignity."

Sunday Night on the Streets of Albuquerque

It had been a rough day physically. I just didn't feel good, but I figured one surefire way to feel better was to take my mind off how I felt and focus on the needs of others. That evening I would encounter many others during our Joy Junction regular street outreach. On the way to downtown Albuquerque my stomach was doing a dance, so I stopped off at a convenience store to get Pepto-Bismol. Maybe two small orders of fried clams earlier on in the day (comfort food for me) hadn't been the best choice!

It was seventy-nine degrees as I pulled into our downtown parking lot just before nine at night and met up with Lisa Woodward, our transportation manager. The van was loaded with sack lunches and water.

At our first location we found a number of people, including one man who exhibited many of the characteristics of mental illness. We gave him and a handful of other people sack lunches and drove south a bit.

We arrived at our next stop, where we found seven men again unable to find shelter for the night. One man had fashioned a makeshift bed out of a plastic garbage bag he found on the street. Another guy put our empty soup box under his head, while someone else used an old jacket for a blanket. No one else out there had covers or mats. They propped themselves against the wall and gazed at us plaintively.

Some of the men slept with their shoes under their head. This is a theft prevention measure and is usually effective. If one has shoes of the slip on variety, sleepers wouldn't wake up if someone pulled them off while they were sleeping.

As we drove on, Lisa reflected, "Downtown Albuquerque on the weekend—nothing but trouble!" We made our way to an abandoned building where a couple of nights before we spotted an inebriated pair sleeping. No one was there this time, and no signs of their earlier presence remained. We stopped to get coffee.

We moved onto the heart of downtown Albuquerque and fed about a half dozen people. One guy admitted he was homeless but said he didn't need a place to stay because he had a place to camp. He looked very scared and Lisa described him as "a victim waiting to happen." That reminded me how I would feel if I suddenly became homeless again. We talked about trying to find him again to see if we could help, but unfortunately we weren't able to do so.

We drove over to the Fourth Street "mall," apparently now designated as a park, where begging and soliciting are prohibited. Even there, though, it was a pretty quiet night and no one was around. We moved on.

We made our way down a crazily busy Central Avenue, where partygoers were out in force. I wondered why any adults, others than those wanting to cause trouble, would want to go down there. It was a loud and frightening atmosphere, and I wanted to escape from there as soon as possible.

We stopped at a park and gave a number of lunches to grateful people for whom the park would be home that night. One was hitching a ride to Missouri, where he said there was work. He'd eaten little all day and was grateful for the food and encouragement. As a couple of individuals passed by, Lisa encouraged me to return quickly to the van. She identified them as a couple of drug dealers, well known in that area of town, with whom we had no wish to have an encounter.

We made our way back to some of our earlier spots. A few more people had gathered and the refrain was "We're thirsty!" We gave out a variety of beverages and sack lunches and moved on. It was getting close to calling it a night.

While heading back to our parking lot we saw a young woman

carrying a baby. I asked her if she was okay. She said she was. I had doubts, but there wasn't much I could do. I breathed a quick prayer for the two of them, and a couple of minutes later we arrived back at Joy Junction. It was eleven forty-five and seventy-seven degrees outside.

Lisa departed to check on a shelter driver, and I headed back home. With the excitement of the evening's outreach over, my stomachache returned. Apparently, a stomach bug was making the rounds. *Oh well,* I thought as I cranked up the country music. *This too shall pass.*

A Weekend Oasis for the Homeless

Imagine that instead of the weekend being a time of relaxation and rest, it was a time of dread, hunger, and monotony. For a number of Albuquerque's homeless, TGIF is replaced by TGIM (Monday). Some services available in the week close their doors on Friday afternoon until 8:00 a.m. on Monday. People already tired and dispirited have to carry their bags around the city, worrying that if they stop anywhere for long they'll get into trouble for loitering—or maybe even accosted and robbed. Then there is always the pressing problem of finding an available bathroom.

To help address this discouraging situation, Joy Junction is allowing its overnight guests who sign up for a bed Friday evening to stay until Monday morning. This is a fairly new policy, and Joy Junction guests appreciate it very much. Assuring them of a bed for the next night, it helps them get some rest from carrying bags place to place, and it allows them more repose in preparation for the upcoming week.

The policy is one that just makes sense. Why should we have people leave to wander the streets of downtown for the weekend? There are few services available, and as a result our most needy and vulnerable citizens are getting plunged even deeper into the quagmire of homelessness. I hope this new policy will help move some of our guests toward recovery.

Albuquerque's Growing Homeless Problem Needs a Solution

Our struggling economy continues to have a profound impact on New Mexicans. We see professionals out of work, college graduates unable to find careers, and families worrying about making ends meet. Many of these people in need are being forced into homelessness, sleeping on the street, living in their cars, or visiting Joy Junction's mobile feeding unit, the Lifeline of Hope. In some areas during our daily street outreaches around town we see lines of between seventy-five and one hundred people needing something to eat and drink. On night outreach in other areas, we see large numbers of people sleeping on the streets in frightening conditions.

During the economic downturn, Joy Junction has provided New Mexico's homeless with shelter, support, and hope. In 2012, as the state's largest emergency shelter, we were able to provide over 200,000 meals and about 120,000 nights of safe, warm shelter to homeless women, men, children, and families. While this may seem like a large accomplishment, much more remains to be done.

In my twenty-six-plus years serving as CEO of Joy Junction, this current time represents one of the largest ongoing increases in the number of homeless families I have seen. In fact, women, children, and families are one of the fastest-growing segments of the homeless population. When I began Joy Junction, I never had any inkling that the homeless issue would escalate to its present size. While we are helping many, we feel compelled to do so much more.

Think about homeless children for a moment. They don't have a home to go back to after school. Some are living in motels, some staying with relatives and friends, and others live at shelters and rescue missions like Joy Junction. Some are even living out of cars. Some move so often that they have to change schools, miss class, or fail to go to school altogether.

As an article titled "The High Cost of Poverty," published on the website of the National Diaper Bank Network in July 2012, reads, "[Homelessness] fundamentally affects how you are able to function in life. This is particularly true for students ... who often come to school hungry, without enough sleep, and without having done their homework because they lack the supplies and the space necessary to do it."

Our facilities house up to three hundred homeless women, men, and children daily, but we have to turn people away every night because of this increase. The economic downturn has left us with a lack of space and adequate facilities to help New Mexico's homeless. To provide for all those in need during these tough economic times, Joy Junction is planning to expand and renovate its facilities. Currently, we have a multipurpose building that serves as a classroom, a church, a kitchen, a dining hall, and sleeping quarters for some of our guests. It is not big enough, however, for the number of people we serve. We hope to be part of the solution to homelessness in our community by renovating and expanding our campus.

The planned expansion includes a new dormitory with real beds for guests and a new community chapel for classes and church services. Our plans also call for a dedicated women's center that will provide a secure place for women and their children, as well as a vocational training center to teach our guests the skills they need to find jobs and break the cycle of homelessness. With these changes, we can provide more space and service for the homeless in need.

Together we can build a promising future for those in need in New Mexico. As businesspeople, community members, and neighbors, we can come together to find a solution to homelessness in our city.

A Pampered Soul Experiences an Afternoon on the Streets

Joy Junction office manager Barbara Barton describes her life as "pampered," and she says it was a good learning experience spending a recent afternoon on Joy Junction's Lifeline of Hope mobile feeding unit.

"Although a lot of homeless people are not drug addicts or alcoholics, as a society, many of us believe that is why they are homeless. A lot of people also believe that homeless people are dangerous, and are afraid to be around them. I too, at one time, believed these misconceptions about the homeless." Working at the shelter and experiencing an afternoon riding on the Lifeline of Hope has changed some of Barbara's misconceptions.

Recalling an afternoon spent on the Lifeline of Hope, Barbara said that among other things, she was able to experience personally the difficulty homeless people endure every day from the weather. "When we left Joy Junction, it was a sunny and hot day, and the air conditioner in the truck didn't seem to be as cold as I would have liked. Despite the heat and humidity, we continued along the route the driver makes daily."

Barbara said every time the truck pulled into a different location the driver would honk her horn and drive around the area to alert people that the truck was there with what may be their only meal of the day. By the time the Lifeline was parked, Barbara said, there was already a line of people anxiously awaiting food, drinks, and personal hygiene items.

Barbara continued, "Many of the people we served were children, which made me wonder why they were getting food for the parents and why the parents themselves didn't come out. I wondered if they were too sick, hung over, or maybe passed out. My heart broke for them wondering if there was anyone responsible watching these young children."

At one of the Lifeline's busiest stops, in an economically challenged area of southeast Albuquerque, Barbara told me there were a lot of homeless people already awaiting the truck's arrival. "By the time we parked, the crowd seemed to have doubled from out of nowhere. There was a gentleman there who said he was just released from prison that day and had nowhere to go. Our driver then gave him one of our business cards and told him about our life recovery program."

After they handed out food and beverages, someone wanted to pray. "So we formed a circle and JodiLynn Bartell [a Joy Junction driver] said a very beautiful prayer, which seemed to put a smile on everyone's faces as they walked away."

By the time the crew arrived at another location, Los Altos Park, the winds and rain came, and the temperature outside got chilly. "Despite the weather," Barbara said, "some of the homeless people were still sitting on the cardboard boxes they call beds laid out in the park. They were excited to see us and told us about the problems they had encountered the night before with another homeless person, which they joked and laughed about. They did not seem to be afraid, and the weather didn't seem like much of a concern, either."

As they were leaving the park, Barbara said someone told them that skaters at a nearby skate park had harassed the homeless group and that "if anything should happen to them for us to look for the skaters."

As the Lifeline of Hope outreach drew to a close for the day and the team drove back to Joy Junction, Barbara said, "I thought about all the people we had left in the sweltering heat and then the wind and rain, but to my amazement not one of all the people we saw said a word about the weather. I spoke to some of them, and the people I met were very cordial and polite. My experience on the Lifeline changed the way I look at the homeless. I just wish there was a way we could do more to help them and show that we care about them."

Barbara said that while she had a "sick feeling in the pit of her stomach" about the amount of need in Albuquerque, there was much more to it than that. "At the same time, I had a sense of peace knowing that we had given them not only food and drink, but also a smile and an understanding that there are those who do care for them. It was a very enlightening experience to me, and I would love to be able to go out with the Lifeline of Hope more often."

An Afternoon on Joy Junction's Lifeline of Hope

On this wet, damp, and cold day, the Lifeline was again making its way across Albuquerque. It was a sad day, for along with the rest of the nation, we were hearing about the tragic school shootings in Connecticut.

Our first stop was outside Healthcare for the Homeless in downtown Albuquerque. Our driver pulled up with anticipation over being able to help a population she knows all too well, having been homeless once herself. The Lifeline was loaded with sack lunches, hot food, blankets, personal hygiene items, and more. To the backdrop of an increasingly ominous sky, whatever supplies we could manage for the homeless and hungry were such a blessing.

There were about fifty-five people lined up, including a man in a wheelchair. Our driver introduced me to a man from England who said he'd like to join our life recovery program. Though he'd been there ten years, he still spoke with a very pronounced English accent. We called the shelter and arrange a pickup.

We also served a man from New York, a woman from Mexico, veterans, and families with infants. What does the Lifeline of Hope offer? Just that: hope—regardless of who the individuals we serve are. One of our staff got the "warm fuzzies" as she bantered with a vet about football. She was also excited to see that even the homeless do what they can to "represent" their favorite teams. She discovered what anyone discovers when visiting with the homeless: they are really no different than you or I.

The friendly banter brought out much laughter. A guy came up and patted me on the back and asks me how I'm doing. *How am I doing? How is* he *doing?* I wondered. I asked him where he was staying, and he said, "Outside." I say, "You know we can help you, right?" He said, "Thanks. I know. But it's not that severe yet."

Not that severe yet? Really? It felt way cold to me. My fingers got increasingly cold typing my notes on my BlackBerry.

The same guy told me happily he had sold a couple of paintings. I wondered what his story was. I didn't feel comfortable asking right now.

Another guy came up, smiling, and said, "Hello, Mr. Joy Junction." I shook his hand and he went to get his meal.

A man arrived and asked for a sack lunch. Our driver, who had an obvious rapport with clients, asked him, "Where's your girl?" "Visiting our kids," he replied with a smile.

The sky was turning bluer, but it was still far too cold to be outside for any length of time. My mind returned to Connecticut. What a world we live in!

A guy asked for an extra lunch, and we were happy to oblige.

We offered someone some hot food. He shook his head mournfully and said, "Oh no, I don't have a way to keep it hot. Don't you have burritos?" "Yes." "Okay. I'll have one right now." We bantered a little, and he left with a big smile on his face.

Hygiene items, such as deodorant, toothbrushes, and toothpaste, were much-requested items. A woman came up to me, offered her assistance at Joy Junction, and said, "I love your accent." Funny, I didn't think I had one anymore.

We headed to a hotel in a differently deprived part of southeast Albuquerque, where we served another kind of homeless clientele: folks who have to decide between paying for a room for the night or having a warm meal.

As we approached our next destination the sun forced itself through the clouds. We could feel the heat, and I'm sure the people on the streets were grateful for this temporary rush of warmth. I hoped our Lifeline did the same for them.

The Lifeline pulled in just behind us, honking to let people know we had arrived. A line of people formed, including some youngsters. They excitedly ran up and asked for a sack lunch. As our driver gives one to each of them we heard a chorus of thank-yous.

The line grew longer, and a man politely asked for a loaf of bread. We had a number of loaves, thanks to the kindness of a local grocery chain. Then another man, dressed in Santa Claus red and clutching his hot food and beverages, asked for his sack lunches. He got all he wants and walked off.

Someone asked for a jacket. "Hold on a minute," our driver replied. They moved over and waited.

I started thinking of the Connecticut shootings when a couple with a young child asked me if I heard about the tragedy. It was almost as if they were reading my thoughts. I nodded sadly.

There was a man hobbling on crutches. The need of everyone in our line was almost overwhelming. More people came. My shivering fingers continued tapping away on the BlackBerry while our driver serves clients, many of whom greeted me by name. They were so appreciative.

One woman was there with a short-sleeved shirt. I asked her if she was cold, and she smiled, said yes, and walked quickly back to her room. Another woman gave us two dollars. I told her that it was not necessary, but she insisted on me taking it, saying we had helped her a couple of years ago when she was evicted from her apartment. She told a man asking for food and looking for his pregnant wife that she hadn't seen her. He said, "She's pregnant. I'm not!" The banter continued.

Not only did we serve the people staying at this hotel, but I noticed that families from a nearby trailer park made their way to the back of the line to receive food.

Soon it was time to leave. Before the next stop, which was in a troubled, busy, and dangerous location, we stopped for a cup of coffee and a homemade tortilla. As we entered through the restaurant doors, the heat infused my shivering fingers and bones. How the homeless stay outside for hours and hours and days on end really is beyond me.

We arrived at our next location, where a line of about fifteen souls quickly formed. They included a middle-aged woman pushing a shopping cart and a man in a wheelchair. Our Lifeline crew handed out supplies as people continued waiting patiently in line.

Parked just across the lot from us was a harm reduction van, where clean needles and condoms are provided. While harm reduction is a controversial practice in some circles, to me it's a good thing. How can you preach the gospel unless you keep someone alive?

A man walked up pushing a shopping cart with a trash can perched on top. On the front of the cart there was a suitcase and a box with a broom handle. I wondered what the story was here. Could you imagine living like that? I couldn't.

My car thermometer showed me it was forty-four degrees outside. People stood by the Lifeline eating burritos and drinking beverages. I saw a man putting two burritos in his pocket and walking off. Where to, I wondered? Life for many homeless, hungry, and poor people consists of waiting and walking, often to nowhere!

Two couples walked off hand in hand.

A car pulled up and dropped off a man who joined the line for food.

What would these people do without the food and supplies offered by the Lifeline?

As we gave out blankets, there were a lot of delighted smiles. How appreciative will you be of your blankets and bed covers tonight?

The Lifeline closed up shop, and it was time to move onto our next stop, a seedy, low-rent motel frequented by the homeless. It was getting dark, and we still had a couple more stops to go.

We arrived, and the Lifeline honked. It was a small but cheerful crowd here. One guy quipped, "You guys ready for this cold snap?" Some of our clients here were not really ready for the cold weather and shivered while in line. We fed them as fast as we could. I could already feel the biting cold whip through my jacket.

A man came out of his room with bare feet. He was so grateful for the food he and his girlfriend received from the Lifeline. It was heartwarming. He excitedly told me that he stayed at Joy Junction for a year and graduated from our Christ in Power life recovery program.

He went on to say that although he was not working full-time, he was working four days a week. His broken English didn't stop him from telling me his great story. It's stories like his that keep me motivated.

We pulled into the last location. A guy with a nasty cough came out wearing a T-shirt. We served him quickly, and he moved slowly back to his room.

I heard a man arguing with the motel manager, trying to get his money back. He said he'd paid for a few nights, but he was on his way to jail. The exchange got a little heated. I don't know if he got his money back or not, but it looked doubtful. The man turned to us and asked if the food was free. We assured him it was, but he didn't come over. He just kept arguing with the manager.

As things seemed to be escalating I decided it was time to pull my team out of the area. The great thing is that we fed everyone we'd seen who was in need. We had served 250 hot meals and 170 sack lunches, and we gave out a number of blankets and personal hygiene packs. They were all delivered with lots of love and smiles.

All of this activity represented an afternoon on Joy Junction's Lifeline of Hope. Please pray for the successful continuance of this ministry of compassion.

A Very Special Time at Joy Junction: CIPP Graduation

Joy Junction is typically thought of as being a homeless shelter, a place where needy people can find a place to stay and enjoy a warm, nourishing meal. While that is very important, there is much more to it than that. While we shelter and feed people and provide an array of other services, we also offer a nine-month faith-based life recovery program called the Christ in Power Program, or CIPP.

CIPP participants are taught the skills they need to reenter and succeed in the workplace. They learn, for example, anger management, healthy eating habits, resume writing, and a variety of important coping mechanisms.

A few weeks ago, we had a ceremony for thirteen program graduates. Some of them shared how the program had touched their lives. Frank said the graduation ceremony gave him a feeling of respect and more. It taught him to keep on going, even when the going got hard. "When doing something to better myself, I've learned not to give up, but to always go forward. Even if it is hard, I need to continue what I started. Now that I have graduated, I know I can achieve and accomplish what I thought was too hard."

Andrea said, "Graduation meant seeing a number of people working together to reach a goal to overcome addictive behaviors." She said God helped her successfully graduate from the program, and so did the other program participants.

For Deana, CIPP graduation was very important, as it was only the third time in her life that she had successfully followed through to the conclusion of a goal. "It meant a sense of accomplishment. Going through this nine-month program, completing it, and graduating made me feel like I can accomplish anything I set my mind to. It also gave me a sense of pride, because I saw my friends and family's faces, and I knew they were proud." Deana said it wasn't an easy program. "There were many times I wanted to quit. But I stuck it out and made it through. So going through this graduation helped me realize what a strong person I have become. I stuck it out for nine months, and I am a better person today because of this program and the staff here at Joy Junction."

Our other life recovery program participants who have yet to graduate were also in the audience. The ceremony touched Louis. He said when he graduates it will mean "the completion of a goal and the beginning of a new phase in my life." He added, "Dr. Reynalds has found a way through our Lord to make Joy Junction a shelter every other mission in America should emulate. The CIPP program has not only saved me but changed my life completely. For someone who has been agnostic his entire life to be saying what I say now about my belief in Jesus as my Lord and Savior proves that if you want your life bad enough, this program works. You just have to want it and have a little faith."

Barbara said when she graduates our life recovery program, she will have "the knowledge and resources to continue on a path of sober living and a change of lifestyle." She also said, "Completing the twelve-step program will help me earn the respect of my children as they are also hurting as a result of a broken family and separation. This will help my marriage and getting my family back together."

Caroline said that her graduation will mean "my heart and soul have been filled with the love of God. I will be able to accomplish anything that I set out to do. I will feel like I can face and conquer the world with my head up and with a smile on my face."

The graduation ceremony was a wonderful experience, and God's presence and blessing was evident. Would you pray for all our graduates, as well as those who are still making their way through the Christ in Power Program?

A Day in the Life of Joy Junction's Kitchen Manager

Overseeing the production of thousands of meals monthly is not a job for the faint of heart! It is especially challenging when the bulk of what you serve comes in as donations throughout the week. Yet that is the gargantuan task faced by Donald Ravizza, kitchen manager for Joy Junction. He recently took some time to tell me about his typical day.

Don usually arrives at Joy Junction just before five in the morning. This day was no exception, and he wondered what lay in store. "As I parked my car, I wondered if I would have enough food on hand to serve everyone. Before I entered the building, I checked the walk-ins outside to see what kind of donations we received the previous night. There was a variety." Don said that as he entered the building it became apparent we had yet again experienced God's blessings. There was enough bread to make it through yet another day.

"Next I checked the reach-ins to see if we had gotten any meat donations. Again God had blessed us—lots of meats, whole chickens, hamburger patties, even some steaks."

Don added, "I usually vary from serving hot and cold cereal and pancakes during the week, to eggs, French toast, bacon, or sausage (if we have any) on the weekends. Our residents get an extra hour to sleep in on the weekends, which gives my staff more time to do a nice, hot breakfast."

Don's next concern was whether he would have enough staff for the day to get the job done. Wanting to give some of Joy Junction's former guests an opportunity to build an employment resume, the shelter provides jobs for some of them in various departments, including the kitchen. At times, however, that can be a challenge. Today, for example, Don said, "I found out the cook needed to leave at 9:00 a.m. for a court date. And I'm not complaining, but we always seem to be shorthanded for one reason or another. Either a forgotten appointment, illness—it's always something. We always get through the day somehow, though."

With breakfast out of the way, Don focused on putting away the donations that came in last night. There was a lot of produce and meat. It didn't take very long, and once that was done, he focused on snacks. "We generally do a snack for the life recovery class at the halfway point. It gives the residents a chance to stretch and have a cup of coffee and a pastry. We had a good assortment today. Some days, it's slim pickings, but our residents appreciate whatever we can provide all the same."

Next, Don and his crew moved on to lunch. The menu was tacos, Spanish rice, beans, Mexican pastries, and soda. That, he said, turned out to be a crowd pleaser. "Prep for lunch went off without a hitch. What we prepared was well received, and our residents seemed to enjoy it."

No sooner than lunch is over is it time to think about dinner. Don combined tri-tip roasts with mashed potatoes, vegetables, and bread. He was happy with the way his cook was grilling the steaks—"the way I like them. If you slightly undercook them, pan them, and place them in the warmer, they come out a perfect medium by service time. We decided on mashed potatoes for tonight, as we did rice pilaf last night. We were almost out of potatoes, but more typically come in from generous donors in the week."

"We were able to get dinner on time," Don said, "even though our crew was down two. It just meant we had to work a little bit harder. The thing that gets me through most days here is knowing that what we do is truly helping someone in need. I have been pretty blessed in my life and truly enjoy what I do here."

A highlight of Don's work at Joy Junction? He said one would have to be when one of our guests approached him a few weeks ago and said Don had raised the food quality to that of a five-star shelter!

As the day came to an end for Don, it was "another one in the books. Everyone we fed hopefully enjoyed it, and now I'm going to head home and get ready to do it all over again tomorrow."

An Unscheduled and Extraordinary Day

There are never two days alike in my job as the CEO of Joy Junction. While I have scheduled meetings, sometimes the unscheduled activities make the day. Take last Wednesday, for instance.

It began with some routine work at my home office, followed by a lunch with my assistant, Kathy Sotelo, and a Joy Junction friend who wanted to talk about a fundraising opportunity for the shelter.

After that, there was a scheduled meeting with a company on the far southwest side of Albuquerque. An employee there had put together a blanket, food, and clothing drive and wanted to talk about volunteer opportunities at the shelter. Before this meeting and during our lunch, however, I received an e-mail from our office. A Good Samaritan had called in with a concern. She saw a person with a cart staying in some bushes close to a hotel in Albuquerque's Northeast Heights neighborhood. The caller said the person's cart hadn't moved for two or three days, and she was afraid the individual may be in bad shape in the bushes. Our office manager told her to call local law enforcement but said she would pass the message on and see if we could go check things out.

We were happy to do so. We left the restaurant and made our way to the location, where we spotted a couple of shopping carts. Kathy stayed in our parked car, because if someone was there, we didn't want to scare him or her. There was a mass of belongings strewn all over the ground, but no one was immediately visible.

I looked closer. Sticking out from under a blanket was an arm with a bandage wrapped around the hand. There was something about the way it looked that caused my heart to pound. I spoke softly. "I'm from Joy Junction. Are you okay?"

No answer. I motioned for Kathy to join me. As soon as she observed the arm, she had the same feeling I did. Was this person dead? But a few seconds later a voice responded, "Hello."

It was a woman, and again I asked her if she was okay. Without moving much she said she was. I asked her if she was hungry. She sat up a bit, pulled the blanket over most of her face, and said she would like some food. We said we would be right back and went to a fast-food restaurant a few hundred yards away. We bought her a couple of burritos and (at her request) a diet drink.

She talked a bit as she ate. She was okay and had recently been checked out by paramedics. She was quick to reassure us that all her vital signs were fine. I asked her if she had a place to stay. She said she did, at a friend's house.

Kathy asked her name, and when she told us, we recognized her as someone long homeless in Albuquerque whom various agencies over the years had unsuccessfully tried to help. She just couldn't follow the rules or fit into the structure of a homeless shelter. As we prepared to leave, I told her we would pray for her. She quickly told us in response that she had her Bible and would pray for us too. Looking at her situation, as you can imagine, that was unbelievably touching and very poignant.

We told her good-bye and left for our next meeting. As I looked at the time, I realized we were running somewhat late, so Kathy called the person we were meeting with and explained the situation, and we made our way across town. The meeting with the man who did the food and clothing drive for us went well. As we talked to our "new" friend, I quickly realized he wasn't really new to Joy Junction at all. This man and his wife were long-time supporters of our work. We talked about volunteer opportunities available at Joy Junction and how employees at this company could be of assistance to Albuquerque's homeless population. Driving back into town, I was reminded again of the many friends and supporters the Lord has given us at Joy Junction. I said a quick prayer of thanks. What blessings! What encouragement!

Next on the agenda was a networking meeting sponsored by the Albuquerque Chamber of Commerce. We had an hour or so before the event was scheduled, so we made a stop for coffee to catch up on phone calls and e-mails. The chamber meeting was held that night at a local toy store, and Kathy and I held forth on our needs and victories at Joy Junction. Everyone to whom we spoke expressed appreciation for what we do on behalf of our city and its homeless.

It was now time for me to meet with volunteer community liaison Erika Ferraro, a regular participant on our Lifeline of Hope and various other Joy Junction outreach activities. We were wrapping up the evening when we ran into a couple and their dog who were stranded in Albuquerque. We learned they were from Las Vegas and had been locked out of their motel room for an inability to pay. As the man described the couple's plight, tears began running down his cheeks. It was obvious he was very scared.

We encouraged them, but they still needed a place to stay. With a dog, staying at Joy Junction was not realistic. I told them we would pay for the remainder of that night's room rent, as well as one more night to give them a little more breathing room. I then arranged for our van to pick them up and take them back to their motel. I also told our van driver to bring some sack lunches for the couple. They left much happier than when we met them. We then drove to their motel, just a short distance from where we met the couple (but a long way, if you're walking), and settled their tab.

It was now about nine forty-five, and as Erika left for home, I drove over to check in at Joy Junction to make sure everything was okay. I chatted with Harold Eansor, our evening receptionist, and then made my way home. I went up to my home office, where I answered some of the e-mails I hadn't had the opportunity to care for in the day.

At about eleven thirty I called it a night and turned on the TV to watch the news. That was one day as the CEO of Joy Junction. Tomorrow will be another one. There are never two days alike in my job. The only constant is that my BlackBerry always stays with me at all times—kind of like a lifeline for my sanity.

A Day in the Life of the Resident Services Manager at Joy Junction

Can you imagine a job that is a spiritually and emotionally fulfilling calling but is nevertheless totally draining? That describes the position of Joel Steen, the resident services manager at Joy Junction. If he had a typical day, what would it look like? He told me about one.

Joel pulls up to the gate at Joy Junction about eight o'clock each morning. As usual, he rolled down his window this morning to greet the guard shack attendant. But no one came. "I honked, thinking sometimes they don't hear my quiet vehicle. There was still no response. Now I was wondering what was happening," Joel said.

The guard shack attendant is an essential position at Joy Junction. It's one of the volunteer positions in our life recovery program. While every position is an important part of the shelter's life recovery program, the guard shack attendant must be available at all times while on shift to help ensure the safety of our residents.

Joel said this was the first day in over a year that he had come to work at Joy Junction when the guard was absent from the gate. Joel said, "I got out of my car and checked the guard shack myself. The door was wide open, but no one was home. Immediately I called John, the floor supervisor on duty. He was unaware of the situation, but sent out Melissa to cover as the attendant until we could find out what happened. I continued on to the office, clocked in, and met with John."

About ten minutes later, the truth came to light. The young man who was on duty as the guard shack attendant made an error in judgment, thinking he could leave for a few moments. He was reassigned to a different, less vital position. Joel said, "I knew I'd have to find someone else to fill his place. I decided to send him to see the Joy Junction chaplain. I knew a bit about his family situation, and I knew he was struggling."

This was going to be a busy day, and Joel thought about what was coming up. First off, there was the managers meeting at ten and then right after that the supervisors meeting at eleven. He had to prepare for both of these while also checking his e-mail. There were a few "flagged" items, which he went to work on. One was from a donor who wanted to help one of the shelter residents with an apartment. This was very important, so Joel called him immediately. He then called a state of New Mexico adult protective services worker regarding a Joy Junction resident. Then he answered an e-mail from one of his floor supervisors.

Three clicks, three flags unchecked. Now it was time to start preparing for those meetings. While most people dread office meetings, Joel actually looks forward to them. For him, "It's a chance for us all to get caught up, to work through issues and victories with our CEO, and to laugh a little. Sometimes we laugh a lot. We need to. This day was no exception."

Joel walked into the office of Jennifer Munsey, Joy Junction's COO, for the managers meeting. He sat down warily next to Lisa Woodward, Joy Junction's transportation manager. Why "warily"? Joel mused, "Months ago, for some reason, I earned the moniker 'kitty cat.' Could it be my short-cropped hair? My salt and pepper beard? My demeanor? Whatever it was, I have since found litter box scoops and kitty scratching posts on my podium between classes. I have also been made to dance publicly to the Disney ditty 'We Are Siamese.' I never know what may crop up next."

According to Joel, the managers meeting went well, and Joy Junction would run more smoothly because of it. The meeting didn't go off without *any* hitches, however, as occasionally Lisa tried to flick at Joel's ear just to bother him. Joel returned the favor by poking at her hand with his pen. Joel and Lisa were not the only culprits. After the closing prayer, Robert Batrez, Joy Junction's maintenance manager, grabbed Lisa's foot and wrestled off her shoe. Then he gave the shoe to Joel, who took it outside the office and placed it in the lost and found. Lisa, now hobbling around, threatened retaliation for the theft. Finally Joel returned to the office with the shoe and tied it onto the doorknob. Jennifer lent a hand by taking pictures to memorialize the occasion.

And that was one of the more sedate managers meetings. You may wonder what place such antics have in a rescue mission—and a Christian ministry at that. I have a simple answer for that. Sometimes being appropriately goofy gives us the ability to keep on keepin' on and remain in this ministry of compassion for the long haul. As with any mission, we deal on an ongoing basis with lots of stress and a variety of crisis situations. The activities Joel described are wonderful tension relievers. They also provide an opportunity for our staff to bond and just enjoy being appropriately silly.

Next for Joel on this busy day was the resident supervisors meeting. He said, "Like the managers meeting, it helps keep each of us focused on our primary objective, which is to serve the homeless, especially families, women, and children, as Jesus would."

A number of things came up for discussion during the meeting, including a sobering story from Joy Junction Chaplain Gene Shiplet. At Joy Junction's annual Thanksgiving dinner at the Albuquerque Convention Center, a homeless man came up to Gene. He said he had eaten his entire meal, but had saved a single piece of pie for later because it would be his only food for the remainder of the day. How tragic!

A new floor supervisor spoke about how she herself was homeless from the ages of fourteen to nineteen. She said, "I'm just so happy to be here." Joel reported that her short testimony brought some to tears.

Following the meeting, Joel enjoyed a quick lunch with another one of our resident supervisors. As Joel walked back to his office through the multipurpose building, Cheryl, one of Joy Junction's life recovery program participants, caught up with him. Joel said her eyes showed the depth of her concern, and he asked her how he could help.

Cheryl blurted out, "I can't take it any longer. I want to be moved to a different shift." Joel probed a little and learned that she was having difficulty working with another individual on her volunteer shift as a programmer. "Give me a little time," Joel responded. "I need to take care of something, but I'll be back to help."

A short time later, Joel met with a state of New Mexico Children, Youth, and Families Department in-home services provider and one of the couples on the shelter's life recovery program. Joel shared with the in-home services provider some details about the program. "She was concerned that the couple be able to leave the Joy Junction property in order to visit their little one. How would that affect their program? I told her that our rules are meant to help and not hinder people. We would make it work. Both she and our couple were happy."

Back to the worried programmer. Joel asked Cheryl into the floor supervisor's office while the supervisor was taking care of other issues. "All my life," she told Joel, "I've never amounted to anything. When I made second lead [on my volunteer shift], I was happy. Now Maria is putting somebody else in my place."

Joel told her, "In cases like these, it's so important that we communicate. Maria may not know exactly how you feel. Would you be willing to try to work it out with me present?" She agreed, and Joel recalled thinking, *Good. We may be able to keep a rift in relationships from happening.*

Maria arrived, and they both took their seats in front of the supervisor's desk. Joel began by telling them, "Here is how this works. We allow each party to speak without interruption or comment. When finished, I will guide us from there. Okay?"

Cheryl began. She told the story of her heartache at being demoted. Joel made sure she was finished before signaling Maria.

"There is no punishment here," Maria began. "You are still part of my team. I put Pam in that position because she has a lot of experience." Beyond that, Maria added that she felt Cheryl needed less stress because of her family situation.

There was silence for a moment. "What do you think, Cheryl?" Joel asked.

"That's fine," she responded.

Joel said to me, "I knew they weren't all the way there, but at least they were on the way. Thanks, God."

Back in his office, it was only a second before Joel heard a knock on his door. It was another programmer, Amanda, whose housing opportunity had fallen through. She was back after only three days away.

Joel said, "What to do with her? At that moment, I wasn't sure. I told her to give me a little time and I would get back to her. Jesus, give me wisdom."

Joel moved onto the next issue. Previously, he had sent a member of our recovery program to a detox facility, since she came to the property drunk. Joel called her in and asked, "Natalie, what happened?"

"I called my mother." She began crying. "I haven't talked to her in three years, and I missed her. But all she did was yell at me. I went and got drunk. It'll never happen again."

Joel offered her a tissue. "That's hard. I'm sorry." They sat for a moment. He continued, "We want to try to help you, Natalie. Of course, you have to live with the consequences of your decisions. I want you to stay in our multi [as opposed to a smaller room] for two weeks. I also want you to stay on property for thirty days." Joel said, "She understood. It was hard for her, but she knew it was better than the streets."

Joel's day wasn't over yet, as he still needed to get back with Amanda, as well as make a supervisors' schedule for the following week. Before doing so, he made a quick call to a probation and parole officer for a previous program participant and left him a message. He also had a brief phone call with a person doing some course work focused on the topic of Joy Junction.

Now it was Amanda's turn. Joel called her in, and they chatted a little about her situation and her goals. He said, "Amanda, you keep flip-flopping between work and apartments, and being on our program. You can't do both at the same time. I want you to spend a week in the multi. Really think and pray about where you want to be and how you're going to get there. Fair?"

She said, "Yes. What do I do in the meantime?"

"What do you want to do?"

Amanda replied, "Finish what I started." She was referring to her volunteer position in the kitchen. He motioned in that direction. "Go and tell Don Ravizza," he said, referring to the Joy Junction kitchen manager.

Joel finished the supervisors' schedule and thought about clocking out. A knock on the door interrupted his thoughts. Should he answer it? It had been a long day, and he really wanted to go home. He opened the door reluctantly, and it was Cindy, a friend of Natalie's. "Thank you," she said, offering her hand. "Thanks for not sending her away."

"I'm glad we could help. That's what we're here for."

"That's all I wanted."

Joel said, "I'm glad I opened the door."

A few minutes later, Joel was finally able to make his way home to recharge his emotional and spiritual batteries. Another day would soon come.

Would you please pray daily for Joel, and for all the issues he faces and the decisions he has to make every day? He needs an overflowing abundance of God's wisdom.

The Lord's Land—and He Rocks It with a Gentle and Firm Hand

A Special Tale about Joy Junction

There is no such thing as a typical day working at Joy Junction. While shifts are routinely busy, there is always an opportunity to encourage someone with the love of Christ. Heartwarming surprises often follow.

Joy Junction transportation manager Lisa Woodward was reminded of that recently as she made her way to the Amtrak station in downtown Albuquerque to pick up a single woman and her child. Lisa told me that whenever she is asked to pick up a new female resident with children, she tries to schedule the short ride back to Joy Junction without a lot of other new and returning residents on board. That's because, Lisa said, "Their situation is already overwhelming enough."

Lisa arrived at the train station and introduced herself to the woman and her approximately eight-year-old girl. She said, "I had country oldies playing softly, and the sun was just beginning to set. The mother began talking to the little girl and caressing her hair, explaining that everything would be fine. The mother encouraged her daughter to remember that 'we are not like those who live at this place where we're going.'" That perception of the difference between "them" and "us" continued even as Lisa pulled through the gate and up the driveway to Joy Junction.

Lisa said she pulled around to the front of our multipurpose building but did not jump out and start unloading the woman's belongings right away as she usually did. Instead, "I turned around in my seat and made eye contact with the young, well-groomed mother. I explained to her I did not want to offend her in any way, and that she of course could ignore the advice I was about to give her. She said she would welcome any help or advice from me."

Lisa began by telling the young woman the short version of her recovery from alcoholism and homelessness. She ended by asking her, "What does a homeless person look like, and how do they act differently from 'us'?" The young lady stammered a little and looked at her little girl. Lisa continued, "I told her of my being homeless and also of many of the staff members here. There is not an 'us' and 'them.' It is just people trying to make it through."

Lisa didn't pull any punches. She said she told the apprehensive new guest, "In a few minutes you're going to walk through those doors, and the thought of homelessness will hit you hard. There will be well-groomed people like yourself, and there will be those who more than likely crawled out from under a newspaper at some point today."

Lisa told her that tomorrow would be better. She said, "The lights will come on in the morning, and the world will seem very different for a few days, but soon you will have conversations with your new neighbors, and you will start looking at this with different eyes."

Lisa said she told the now surprised woman that her young daughter would soon be playing happily with some of the many youngsters who call Joy Junction home. She would meet children like nine-year-old John, whom Lisa described as having Joy Junction "wired." John would tell her daughter about Lees, who, if begged long enough, would e-mail Dr. Reynolds requesting their every wish, right down to a snowball fight.

Lisa said the young woman looked at her with evident surprise and said, "You make it seem like a magic land." Lisa smiled and said, "No. It is the Lord's land, and he rocks it with a gentle and firm hand."

The woman then unbuckled her daughter's seatbelt and told her to grab her toy, as they were home. Lisa said the child responded by saying, "Mommy, you said our home was lost." The mother smiled and said she was taught that a home had four walls, and in the middle was love to hold them up. "We are home," she told her daughter.

As I learned about this very special incident from Lisa, my first thought was *Wow!* I hope you were as blessed by reading this as I was by learning what happened. Will you prayerfully help us ensure that there will be more small miracles like this for many years to come at Joy Junction?

Life Is Still Beginning at Sixty-Seven

Another workday dawns for Joy Junction receptionist and dispatcher Harold Eansor. Like most other workdays, he gets up, makes some coffee, spends time in prayer, watches CNN for a while, checks his e-mail, and then, just before four in the afternoon, heads out the door and over to Joy Junction's front office.

Harold logs on to the computer to begin his workday, which stretches from four to eleven. He says, "The rest of my shift will be a typical workday. I may have some problems, but those are to be expected in any workplace. The bottom line is that I know what this day, tomorrow, and the next day are likely to bring. I have a certainty to my future, and this was not the case sixteen years ago."

In the summer of 1996, on a hot and hazy day, Harold found himself in downtown Albuquerque. He had just gotten off a bus after awakening from a deep, fitful sleep. He said, "I didn't feel all that well. I was looking around, when I suddenly realized I did not know where I was or why I was there. Most importantly, I didn't know who I was."

Harold looked around for a while, gazing at what to him were very strange surroundings, and wondered why he was there. He said, "I was thirsty, parched, but I didn't see anything like a water fountain. My hand was putting a cigarette into my mouth. I guessed I smoked."

After talking to a stranger, Harold made his way to the hospital. "I soon realized that the stranger was the first of many strangers I would meet. I would eventually meet family and friends, but my list of strangers got longer, and I still knew no one."

Harold had no ID on him and very little money. "The doctors and nurses huddled, whispered, and glanced at me suspiciously. I didn't blame them. They were questioning what was going on with me, and I was also wondering the same thing. Time occasionally seemed to be in slow motion, and then two or three hours would rush by and I would still be there, in the bed, literally without a clue."

Harold tried ignoring the fears in the forefront of his thoughts. But they kept rushing in. "My thinking was a jumble of cobwebs, shadows, dark corners, uncertainty, questions, and more questions. I didn't have time to be afraid. Besides, thinking about being afraid was scaring me even more, and I didn't like that."

He didn't know how they did it, but someone found Harold's sister, who lived in Albuquerque. She came to the hospital, where they had a very awkward introduction. "I don't know how it was for her, but for me she was just another strange face among many," Harold said.

"She told me my name was Harold Eansor and I was fifty years old. She said I drank too much, but that I was an all-around good guy. I tried to be positive and upbeat, saying what I expected others to hear. She seemed genuinely concerned for my welfare, but I was still not going to trust anybody. I felt trust would be a weakness when I needed all the strength I had. I was alone, or so I thought."

Even when Harold looked in the mirror, he didn't see himself—"or this Harold dude." He continued, "It was a strange face. It didn't look like either of us. What was I thinking? I had never seen either of us. The face looked back at me with the same questioning expression that I felt. I felt no recognition, only anger."

In fact, anger overwhelmed Harold. He said he felt angry at himself for not remembering and angry at this Harold in the mirror for not being more forthcoming. He was also angry at those who couldn't tell him what had happened or what he should do. He said, "I chastised myself for feeling this way. I didn't want to alarm the hospital staff with an emotional outburst. They might want to send me to a mental health facility, and I wanted to avoid that."

The hospital had no answers for Harold, but they did make arrangements for him to stay at a men's homeless shelter for a week.

His sister wanted to help him but couldn't, as she was downsizing and moving to a much smaller place.

"None of these arrangements bothered me," Harold said, "because I had no expectations, no plans, no goals, and no outlook for tomorrow. Today was about all I could handle, and it was a daunting task indeed." After a week's stay at the Good Shepherd men's shelter, they planned for him to stay at Joy Junction. Harold wasn't thrilled, but that was more a case of him not having any real interest in the plans being made for him. "My only concern was, maybe, where my next pack of cigarettes was coming from, or my next meal, or a change of clothes. I really didn't care about anything else or anyone. I felt guilty about that, but I didn't know what to do about it. I figured I'd let that Harold guy handle it when he got back to the real world, if he ever got back. Where the blazes was he? I wasn't playing with a full deck. Then again, who is? I just didn't care."

Once at Joy Junction, Harold found caring people who were helpful without prying into his situation. "I don't know what else to call it, but *situation* seemed to fit the bill, and I felt guarded about my situation."

At the first church service Harold attended at Joy Junction, the visiting minister told the congregation that the Lord had brought each of them there for a reason, and it was up to them to figure out what that was. Harold said, "The cobwebs started to clear. The dark was becoming light. My mind started racing. Hold on—I know Jesus and Jesus knows me. Why had I been thinking I was alone? The Lord was with me. He had been with me, but I had just forgotten for a while. The world around me started to come into focus. I wasn't lost; I was found. I had a future and a purpose. I just needed to figure out exactly what that was."

Joy Junction invited Harold to join the Christ in Power program, and he agreed. The CIPP would give him time to make plans. When Harold graduated the life recovery program, we offered him a staff position. "I accepted and could not have been happier."

Harold has worked in a number of staff positions during the last fifteen years, and he continues to enjoy being part of Joy Junction. "My memory never did come back, but I have had sixteen years to create new memories. Occasionally I have regrets that my memory stayed hidden, but I don't have any misgivings about the last sixteen years."

Harold says his new life has provided him the opportunity to grow as a man and as a disciple of the Lord. He adds, "I have a very close relationship with the Lord, and this has allowed me to continue to progress even when thoughts of my past situation might cause me anguish."

His drinking? Harold stopped drinking alcohol the day he arrived at Joy Junction, and he also quit smoking six years ago. He said, "None of this would have been possible without the strength of the Lord. I asked for some of his strength to help me succeed, and he provided."

While Harold has passed official retirement age, he says he doesn't feel old. "I am able to work, and Joy Junction has asked me to stay on the payroll. I'll admit I'm a little slower getting out of bed in the morning. I probably don't have the stamina I had thirty years ago, but who does? I hope to work until I don't feel like being a part of Joy Junction. With that in mind, I will probably be here for many years to come."

From Sleeping under a Truck to Being Transportation Manager for a Homeless Shelter

Because Lisa Woodward's parents were blessed in so many ways, she never wanted for anything. Even so, she describes her family as "large and dysfunctional." And during her growing-up years she called herself a "spoiled brat." She wasn't outgoing, but she did well in school, although she failed to exceed in popularity-grabbing activities like cheerleading.

"I didn't want to wear dresses. I was happy in jeans and a pair of boots. Around the tenth grade, I began to rebel. I fell into a group that drank daily, and, in a strange way, I felt I finally fit in." It was within this group that Lisa met a boy with whom she would spend the first half of her adult life. She describes their life from high school until their midthirties as a "big party." They drank from when they got up until they passed out at night.

"The more alcohol he consumed, the higher his temper would go, and his outlets were me and his son. I knew I should leave, but I also knew my family would not agree to it. Their view was 'You wanted him, and now you have him.'"

As the years went on, their lives became a "river of alcohol." Finally, she said, things exploded. "My stepchild went through a window by his father's hand, and finally I fought back. Six hours later I was walking down the road. He was allowed to stay in my home with my family. I was given $1,500 dollars and a verbal death certificate."

Lisa said she walked to the end of the street, where there was a convenience store. She bought a gallon of vodka and cigarettes. She continued walking about a mile up the street, where there was a restaurant whose owner she knew. Now homeless, she said the man allowed her to stay behind the restaurant under an old tractor trailer.

The ground for Lisa's new home was bumpy and hard, so "I looked around and found an old sign with the restaurant's name on it and some cardboard boxes that I broke down to try and soften things up a little. The only belongings I had were the clothes I was wearing, two changes of clothes in a sack, and a sleeping bag. I opened the bottle and drank till I passed out."

The next morning, Lisa realized she was in serious trouble. But she also knew from much experience that after drinking, things generally didn't look so bad. So she hung around. And that was the way it went for almost five weeks.

Describing her schedule, Lisa said, "I would get up early, trying to beat customers to the restroom in the restaurant so I could clean up. After only a few days the customers had become angry with me, making comments like 'Get a job' and calling me lazy. Finally I started washing up in the ditch across the street."

The summer heat was awful, and it was made even worse by all the metal she was surrounded with. In addition, the winds would roar through at night. The rains soon came, soaking Lisa and causing the sign that doubled as her bed to float back and forth under the trailer.

She walked to the store for beer and a dry shirt, but her shirt was soaked in ten minutes, and there was no way to sleep. She couldn't even drink enough to pass out. "I climbed to the end of the trailer, trying to stay dry. It shifted in the wet soil. A steel beam came down, and my legs were trapped," she said. It was early morning before she was found, and rescue was called. An ambulance took her to a local hospital.

At the end of the third day a nurse told Lisa she was being released. Lisa said she told the nurse she had no place to go and no vehicle to get there in any case. The nurse handed her a list of shelters, and Joy Junction was at the top. Lisa called, and an hour later she was at Joy Junction. But she was far from happy.

Lisa will never forget her first night at Joy Junction. There were people all around her, and many were smiling, though she could not understand why. "The volunteers brought me a sack lunch with an egg salad sandwich, signed me in, and showed me to my sleeping area. They also explained that lights-out was at 9:00 p.m. I wasn't hungry or sleepy, but I did want a drink. My new life began."

Over the next few days, Lisa recalled being rude to both staff and volunteers. She woke up angry and went to bed angrier. However, a couple of Joy Junction staff members insisted she join the shelter's Christ in Power Program, which she did. In this program she discovered she could fit in "without being blind drunk."

She said, "I worked my way up the small CIPP ladder quickly and had volunteer assignments with some authority and respect. I poured myself into volunteer duties and my classes. I began making friends and laughing again. I watched sunsets. It had been so long since I had been sober enough to do that and remember the colors—God's colors."

There were some bumps along Lisa's road to recovery. One day she made a number of mistakes that landed her in a supervisor's office. She said she left the office a little while later, angry for almost failing again. That was the one day during Lisa's program that she almost fell off the wagon. "I started to walk to the gate, fully intending to go to the local convenience store and buy a bottle of vodka and sit on the ditch bank until it was empty." What stopped her? A staff member who had also struggled with alcohol saw Lisa walking off with her head down. She caught up with her and saw the signs of problems in her eyes. "She spoke with me about making mistakes and how we could learn from them so they are not repeated, and then she prayed with me. I turned back and went to my room. That day I knew the Lord's love."

The days flew by for Lisa, and she graduated from the program. As she sat there with her fellow graduates, she wondered what she could do now. Right after that, she was offered a position with Joy Junction in the shelter's downtown parking lot. With that assignment came a small apartment at the shelter's transitional living center. Lisa says, "I was thirty-five years old, and this was the first home that was mine that I had earned."

After a couple of months, Lisa was moved to a driving position, and then she moved to the resident services department for a while. "With hard work and prayer and with each move and promotion, my blessings continued to bloom. Staying sober was no longer a daily struggle. With the Lord, I remained able to refuse temptation."

Today, Lisa is Joy Junction's transportation manager, responsible for a fleet of seven vans, a mobile food truck, and six employees. She explains her service this way: "Mostly I serve God by serving those who are in the same situation I was eight years ago. I have the honor of bringing the lost, scared, and hungry to a home."

As Lisa recalls, "Eight years ago I drank myself into a dark, homeless hole. My spirit was dead, and my heart was black with anger. I have had many people ask me why I even talk about those days or admit to them. But now I thank God for them. Every starting point is at the bottom, because without the bottom there is no top. I am nowhere near the top, but now I can see the light."

Lisa has a special request for everyone reading this. She said, "Whoever may read this, please know that each street person you see has his or her story, and if you knew the story, perhaps you would not see them as only bums or drunks. I was a drunk but never a bum. I did not enjoy sleeping on a floating sign. That is why I will work with, and for, the homeless until my last breath—or until we can end homelessness."

Lisa is still watching the sunsets—"God's colors."

To Fear or Not to Fear! That Is the Question

Fears! We all have them, but we're usually reluctant to admit them. In a recent life recovery class at Joy Junction, the instructor asked participants their greatest fears. The answers were enlightening, so in no particular order, here are some of those mentioned.

Some said they feared relapse. While I've never been an addict, I've worked with New Mexico's homeless for over thirty years, so I've gained a little bit of insight into the thinking of alcoholics and chemically dependent homeless people. Many of them fell into the dark abyss of addiction because of an inability to cope with the horrors or rigors of their daily life. Maybe they were struggling with the memories of sexual abuse or the overwhelming feelings of failure, so they turned to drugs or alcohol for momentary relief. Before they knew it, they were addicted, burned through family and friends, and ended up homeless and at Joy Junction. Many who have stayed with us in this situation have found real peace in a relationship with Jesus, but they still feared the pull of addiction and a return to their old habits.

Others said they feared being homeless again after staying at Joy Junction. We do our best to equip all our guests with the ability to cope with a return to the "real" world. While staying with us our guests don't have to worry where their next meal is going to come from or how they will pay the rent or utilities. That leaves them free to focus on their recovery. Still, after graduation from our nine-month program, some continue fearing whether they can put the principles they learned to successful use.

Along the same lines, some Joy Junction guests said they feared "an unknown future." While many find the tools necessary to live a successful and productive life, the scars of addiction have rendered some virtually unemployable. Others have burned relationship bridges so badly that the chance of them being fixed is very unlikely. That leads to an understandable amount of fear and trepidation.

Some participants said they feared rejection and not being loved. We all want to be loved and appreciated. The love of Jesus Christ is a cornerstone of Joy Junction's life recovery program, and we make sure all our participants know about it. When the drugs and alcohol that were used to mask the pain are taken away, there has to be an effective substitute, and a relationship Jesus Christ is the answer we give. There is no other way.

Sadly, rejection comes in all shapes and forms, from our guests experiencing disparaging looks while walking down the street, to our younger guests being laughed at by their peers and adults being rejection from potential employers when they recognize an applicant's address as a homeless shelter.

Some other fears the life recovery class participants noted are fears common to the rest of us, such as the fear of doctors' offices and concerns about another terrorist attack. Who hasn't had these concerns from time to time, especially if we're scheduled for our annual physical or an appointment to diagnose the cause of that pain bothering us for a while?

Another fear that emerged was not being right with God before death. We address that fear a lot at Joy Junction, and we have a very solid answer for it.

While we encourage our guests to work with physicians, psychiatrists, ministers, social workers, and anyone else who can help get their life back on track, the core philosophy of everything we do at Joy Junction is the sharing of the love of Jesus Christ and entering into a relationship with him. The Lord can give our guests certainty of being in a right relationship with him throughout life in this realm as well as in the life to come. He can also give you the same assurance.

I encourage you to pray for our guests and the fears I've mentioned and consider getting involved with Joy Junction.

Too Few Evangelicals Practice the Compassion They Preach

I am an evangelical Christian, although sometimes I am hesitant about using that word because of its negative associations. I prefer thinking of myself as an ordinary person who loves Jesus and wants to spend his remaining days helping people. Not so long ago I would have described myself as a proud, conservative, evangelical, Republican Christian. Now I'm just me, Jeremy Reynalds, conservative in some aspects, liberal in others, and loving Jesus in all.

So what happened? Well, I'm no longer willing to subscribe to the political correctness that dominates so much of evangelical "orthodoxy." To be honest, I don't think some of it is very, well, Christian. Let me explain.

I founded Joy Junction more than twenty-six years ago. We shelter as many as three hundred people nightly and distribute as many as sixteen thousand meals a month. About six thousand of those meals are served on our mobile feeding unit, the Lifeline of Hope, which crisscrosses Albuquerque seven days a week. In addition to the Lifeline meals being potential lifesavers, we also regard this street outreach as an integral part of relationship building.

Many of the people we assist have been hurt both emotionally and physically in unimaginable ways. For example, very recently we offered a man a hygiene kit, which he initially refused. Why? He said, "I get plenty from the trash." But he accepted the kit when I told him he deserved better than that. What had he experienced for him to think he deserved to retrieve things from the garbage like that?

We also gave three pairs of socks to a woman who was outside with bare feet. (We didn't have any shoes with us, or else we would have provided them.) She appeared intoxicated and quite possibly high. While some would disapprove, I believe what we did was something Jesus would have approved of.

Those are just two of the people we have come across recently in our Joy Junction work. It took years for these individuals to get to where they are, and it may take as long for them to get back on their feet. What are they going to do in the meantime? And who is going to care for them? We believe giving hungry and needy people a meal and more is the right thing to do—the Christian thing to do. Sadly, some evangelicals feel that continuing to feed the hungry is "enabling" them. Really? I have yet to hear substantive solutions about what to do with all those people we should quit feeding. I guess the government could do it, but then how loudly would the conservatives be complaining?

And then there is the matter of a definitely controversial tactic called harm reduction. That's the giving of clean needles to drug addicts and condoms to sex workers and others. Like many evangelicals, I used to criticize harm reduction workers as promoting irresponsible sex and illegal drug use. The problem was, I had never bothered to talk with them. Once I did, I found that they are not promoting random sex or drug use. What they are doing is trying to keep hurting people alive until they are ready to seek the recovery they need to stay alive. Shouldn't evangelicals be applauding that? I have said this earlier, and I will say it again: how can you preach the gospel to someone unless you keep them alive?

From my perspective as CEO of a large emergency homeless shelter ministry, something is not smelling so well in evangelical paradise. I believe it is unconscionable not to feed a hungry person or help a sick, addicted, hurting person trying to stay alive. What's wrong with evangelicals? Shouldn't we who say we have been forgiven so much by such a loving God want to share that same love with those in need?

Then the whole charged political atmosphere, with the religious right and religious left, just about drives me to despair. There are evangelical Christians who actually believe that the body politic is the most important determinant of our country's direction. They believe a change in this president or that Congress is going to spell the success or failure of the nation. It seems to me that evangelicals are being coopted by a political party and reduced to a voting bloc. How tragic! Where is God in the picture? Is he in control or not?

There is only one way our country can be changed, and that is that as Christians live out God's Word, quit judging, and focus on two or three litmus-test issues, the world will see that we are Christians by our love. When that happens, profoundly amazing things will come to pass.

What's Ahead for Joy Junction?

The Bible says, "Where there is no vision, the people perish: but he that keepeth the law, happy is he" (Prov. 29:18 KJV). Twenty-six-plus years after founding Joy Junction, I want you to know that my vision remains the same. It is to provide food, shelter, recovery tools, and the love and encouragement of Jesus Christ to homeless, hungry, and distraught families. But my vision is so much bigger than it was at the beginning, as over the last two and a half decades, the need for this ministry has grown exponentially as we have gotten busier than I could have ever imagined.

What are we thinking for the months and years ahead? I'm glad you asked. Some of you may know we are currently in the midst of a capital campaign to renovate and expand our aging facilities. We plan to build a dormitory to ensure that everyone who comes to stay with us has his or her own bed and doesn't have to sleep on a mat on the floor.

We also want to construct a new chapel where we can hold all our church services, Bible studies, and classes for our life recovery program. Currently we hold all of these in our overused multipurpose building, which also doubles as a dormitory at night and as a dining hall area in the day. What a blessing it will be to have a custom-made building set aside for worship and teaching! The chapel will also serve as a community church, open to the public.

In addition to a dormitory and a chapel, we have had an architect design a vocational training center, where participants in our life recovery program will be able to learn computer basics and other skills that can be transferred to the job market, such how to repair cars or do manicures and pedicures. Then, once they graduate from our nine-month program, in addition to gaining a measure of stability, participants will also have a skill to take with them when they leave Joy Junction. That will make it so much easier to get reintegrated into mainstream community life and become stable.

Last but not least, we are planning on building a center exclusively for women and for their children, if they're mothers. Sometimes women have been subjected to such a level of abuse that for a time they are just not able to be in close proximity to men. In fact, the very sight of a man gets their adrenalin rushing. This women's center will be such a helpful tool in their recovery!

All these improvements will be built on our fifty-two acre campus in the South Valley. While we initially hoped to build the entire project at once, it looks like we will have to build in stages, starting first with the dormitory and then the chapel. Not taking into account donated materials and some volunteer labor, we're estimating we will initially need about five million dollars for those two facilities. Of course, that's a lot of money, but we believe that the same God who birthed Joy Junction and has kept us afloat since our inception will also help us gather these funds. We have a website dedicated specifically to this project: www.togetherwecan.joyjunction.org. I hope you will take a look and consider a generous gift.

In addition to the new construction, we're also mindful of the need for an additional mobile food truck to serve as a second Lifeline of Hope. As well as the ten thousand or so meals we serve monthly at Joy Junction, we also provide about six thousand more meals each month (as well as beverages, blankets, sleeping bags, and more) to needy and homeless folks across the city through the Lifeline. Since we first began this venture about three years ago, the need has escalated so much that we frequently run out of food midway through a route. We just can't get any more food on our current truck. When the Lifeline leaves Joy Junction, it does so fully loaded. We are, quite literally, filled to the brim with food and other supplies every time we go out. Would you pray about buying and funding the operation of another Lifeline of Hope?

Our long-range thinking includes potential expansion out of town—and even in other states. We've had a vision for some time to take the Joy Junction model to other cities and set up shelters for homeless families there. While there are more shelters than there used to be for homeless families, they are definitely in the minority. Sadly, it is still much more common for families in need of shelter to be split up. The issue of the lack of homeless shelters for entire families was the focus of an NBC news program that aired in late 2012. Those interviewed all agreed America needs more family shelters.

This is just a peek at what we have in mind. I hope we can count on your prayerful and financial support.

My benediction for you is that you have complete faith in God as you seek to serve the homeless in his name. God has a special blessing for you: "Praise the Lord. Blessed is the man who fears the Lord, who finds great delight in his commands He has scattered abroad his gifts to the poor, his righteousness endures forever; his horn will be lifted high in honor" (Ps. 112:1, 9).

For more information about Joy Junction, please visit our website at www.joyjunction.org or www.facebook.com/jjabq.
I may be contacted at P.O. Box 27693,
Albuquerque, New Mexico 87125.

CPSIA information can be obtained at www.ICGtesting.com
Printed in the USA
LVOW100827300413

331533LV00003B/6/P